HEALTHY S̲ 4 HEALTHY KIDS

IS MY CHILD DEVELOPING OK?

DR. MAURICE LEVY
M.D, M.Sc., F.A.A.P., F.R.C.P (C)

Copyright ©2012 by Maurice Levy. All Right Reserved. The use of any part of this publication, reproduced, transmitted in any form or by any means, electronic, mechanical, photocopying, recording, or otherwise, or stored in a retrieval system, without the prior written consent of the publisher-or , in the case of photocopying or other reprographic copying, a license for the Canadian Copyright Licensing Agency -is an infringement of the copyright law .

First Printing: 2012   Printed in USA .

Library and Archives Canada Cataloguing in Publication

Ordering Information for Canada and USA can be obtained through bookstores or by visiting the website below.

Publisher: Dr. Maurice Levy

ISBN : 978 – 0 – 9877909 – 0 – 3

Healthy Steps 4 Healthy Kids
Is My Child Developing OK?

- Dr. Maurice Levy -

1. Baby and child
2. Health
3. Parenting
4. Development and Behaviour
5. Pediatrics
6. Child rearing

For more information visit
www.drlevy4kids.com

CoNGrATuLATiOnS!!!!

Your beautiful baby has finally arrived.

There is absolutely nothing like watching your baby grow and develop.

ENJOY!!

INTRODUCTION

GENERAL ASPECTS

The first few years are the most important for the child's health and behaviour. The early years set the stages for self-confidence, readiness to learn at school, and overall well-being in life. It is a time of rapid brain growth during which nerve connections are made, the brain differentiates and develops higher functions along with the body's natural growing and maturing stages.

It is estimated that 15-18% of all children experience behavioral or developmental disabilities. Studies show that the better-educated parents are, the earlier problems are identified and the sooner intervention can begin. As a result, the progress and outcome will be better and include improving the child's development and preventing additional concerns (e.g. behavioral issues).

About 70% of mothers in one study expressed behavioral or developmental concerns regarding their child. About 40% report having concerns, but not sharing them with the child's health professional (mainly due to lack of knowledge). In fact, health professionals detect only 30% of these developmental and behavioral disabilities in children. This may be due to a lack of time to complete a formal assessment (especially during a brief visit where a child possibly suffering from ADHD for example, may be obedient and focused); (b) unfamiliarity with screening measures; (c) few states (e.g. USA) regularly include developmental screening as a part of the preschool health care system; and (d) little or no insurance reimbursement for conducting formal tests.

Thus, it is imperative that parents be knowledgeable about their child's development and behaviour. The more you begin to understand and meet your child's needs, the better parent you become!

This book reassures parents by instilling confidence in parenting skills and answers the most common and uncommon concerns often expressed. Parents can feel comfortable knowing that they are educated in a child's development and behaviour and are equipped with the tools to help their child grow as best as possible.

ABOUT THE BOOK

THE BOOK
How it is Written & What it Provides
- The book is written in an **easy, point-by-point format**. Parents do not have the time to read between the lines or look for the answer in a long story. This easy guide is designed to offer direct and clear answers, saving parents lots of time.
- It is a **comprehensive guide** that provides parents with answers to daily concerns, often asked in the pediatric setting.
- The step-by-step guide allows parents to calm, connect and communicate with their little ones from birth to middle school-aged children and beyond.
- The book is full of **practical and useful content** that is applicable to most infants and children; it is **simple yet individualized advice**.
- The **most recent research** (sound scientific evidence) in development and behaviour along with training and professional experience are included.
- Each chapter begins with a general introductory note to better define the issue at hand.
- For each step, situation or problem in development and behaviour, the tools for early identification or warning signs, red flags, what to do or how to enhance development and when to seek help are provided.
- Although the information provided in this book equally applies to both sexes (i.e. he or she), each sex is alternated through the chapters to prevent the awkward use of "he/she". If a particular problem is related to one sex more than the other, it is explicitly stated. Otherwise, it is equal to both sexes without the intent of offending.
- Essentially, this book is a useful guide that benefits parents and health professionals with multiple pictures, tips and variations that make it concrete and memorable.

Different Sections of the Book
The book contains 4 sections:

Section 1: Developmental Milestones & Ages
- For each specific age for the first 6 years of life, chapters in this section include (a) developmental milestones in the domains of physical, social-emotional, cognitive, speech and language, self-help and adaptive skills; (b) parenting and discipline aspects; (c) how to enhance development; (d) developmental screen checklists and red flags; and (e) other related parent concerns, written in the form of questions and answers.
- Various related tips and "more to know" sections are spread throughout each chapter.

Section 2: Important Motor Developmental Milestones
- These include chapters such as head control, rolling over, sitting, crawling, standing and walking.
- Chapters will describe when and how these develop, how to enhance, causes of delay and when to seek professional help.

Section 3: Recognition of Warning Signs / Symptoms of Developmental Difficulties/ Disabilities
- This section includes the most common disabilities of particular concern. It provides parents with early red flags, warning signs or symptoms that could be associated with a specific disability such as ADHD, Autism, learning disability and speech and language delays.

Introduction to Developmental Milestones

Children develop skills in six broad categories called **developmental milestones**. These skills are acquired within a specific time frame. Although there are variations in developmental patterns, the further away a child is from the average, the less likely he is normal.

Categories of developmental milestones include the following:

1) **Gross motor skills**: These are physical skills including the use of large proximal muscles such as those involved in head stabilization, trunk, limbs and postural control.

2) **Fine motor skills**: These physical skills involve the child's ability to use small muscles, specifically their hands and fingers. It requires a high degree of coordination of predominantly distal muscles and the ability to isolate movements and parts of movements (e.g. building a tower of cubes at 16-24 months).

3) **Social-emotional development**: This is the child's ability to interact with others including helping, sharing, self-control, eye contact, social smiles, aggression, compliance, relationships, feeding, attachment, development of temperament or behaviour styles, independence and autonomy, cooperation and interactive play.

4) **Cognitive skills**: These include thinking skills such as learning, understanding, problem solving, reasoning, memory, attention and imitation. A broad range of skills including auditory and visual discrimination are involved in the development of cognitive skills. Also, cognitive development depends on a variety of experiences in the world through the senses and motor exploration.

5) **Speech and language**: This is the child's ability to both understand (receptive speech) and use language (expressive language). Language and speaking abilities include speaking, using body language, gestures, communicating and understanding others.

6) **Self-help and adaptive skills**: These include eating, dressing, toileting, and hygiene, chores, grooming and learning in social settings. Adaptive skills are sensitive to environmental factors and depend on parents providing opportunities for children to learn these skills.

Multiple factors influence development. These include genetics, environmental, cultural and socio-economic factors, general health, and temperamental characteristics, prematurity and individual differences. Some examples of these differences may include:

(a) Cultural expectations: African infants routinely surpass American infants in the rate of learning to sit and walk, but not climbing stairs or crawling.

(b) Individual differences: Motor ability depends in part on the child's weight and build. After the infancy period, normal individual differences are affected by opportunities to practice, observe and be instructed on specific movements.

(c) Socio-emotional domains: Social and emotional development are influences by environmental learning experiences. However, some evidence suggests a biological basis for certain early social and emotional behavior.

Developmental Checklists & Red Flags

- Developmental screens help determine whether an infant/child is progressing well. The screens are checklists that require a yes or no answer to developmental questions.
- Red flags outline a range of functional indicators or domains that identify potential problem areas for children.
- Each checklist includes various domains of child development in the areas of physical skills, cognitive skills, social-emotional development, speech and language along with hearing, vision, self-help and adaptive skills.
- These checklists help parents and caregiver know what to expect from a child at a specific age and identify early warning signs in order to be referred to a health professional in a timely manner for further developmental assessment.
- As with any screening test, accuracy, sensitivity and specificity can be low. Thus, repeated administration will lead to high detection rates. The screenings cannot contain every possible indicator of developmental limitation, though general goals are met.
- Screenings are not meant to substitute professional advice. Parents should always discuss concerns with the child's health professional.
- Comment: The screen is not a diagnostic tool. Though, it can facilitate discussion regarding development. Any "no" response deserves further clarification and possible action. More than 1 "no" response requires a referral for further assessment. The absence of a single skill at a particular age is rarely sufficient to determine developmental stage. Developmental functions can be emergent, latent (not yet measured), delayed, deficient or disordered.
- Since development is affected by numerous factors (both biological and environmental), repeated screening allows information to be gathered and compared over time; this maximizes the effectiveness of these screens and should be completed at regular intervals.
- Parents and other caregivers (e.g. day care teacher) are also important judges of behaviour and other developmental skills; they may be the first to note any problem.

DISCLAIMER

Despite the fact that the best efforts have been made to ensure that this book is detailed and very practical, and in most cases, will fit your child's case, you must always work in concert with your child health professional. This is because your doctor knows your child's unique needs and over time, recommendations may change or differ according to individual consideration.

The contents of this book are not intended and should not be taken as a substitute for your doctor's advice. It is meant purely for informational purposes. Anything contained in this book should not be considered as specific medical advice with respect to any specific condition and/or person. It is meant to ease your concerns and give you knowledge that complements the information your health professional provides.

Thus the author respectfully and specifically disclaims any liability, risk (personal or otherwise) that may be incurred as a consequence (directly or indirectly) from the use or application of any of the information provided in this book.

For more information and parenting books published by Dr. Levy, please visit:

www.drlevy4kids.com

Dedication

In Loving Memory & Dedication to,
My parents, Jacob & Heftzibah Levy who gave me life and taught me how to persevere in it. To my in-laws, Joseph and Fani Hazan who have always supported my endeavors.

To my beautiful wife,
Brigitte, who is always supportive, understanding and loving in my professional life.

To the joys of my life,
My four children, Lital, Liran, Roy and Jonathan for their support and patience during the writing of this book.

Special thanks:

My eldest daughter *Lital*, for her tireless efforts to transform my ramblings and lengthy details into the simple and easy to read, wonderful book you have before you.

My youngest daughter *Liran*, for her patience and dedication to transform the edited pieces into the colorful designs and lovely photographs you have before you.

Thank you to all the health professionals for their insight and interest in providing me with all their helpful comments and suggestions in support of the development of this book.

ACKNOWLEDGEMENTS

I wish to acknowledge and offer my sincere appreciation and thanks to all those who have provided invaluable feedback and comments on this book including the following psychologists, physicians and other health professionals.

Danielle L. Piver, PhD (Buffalo, New York)

Dr. K. Haka-Ikse, Associate Professor of Pediatrics, University of Toronto and the Hospital for Sick Children (Emer), Toronto, Ontario.

Dr. John Hsuen, Associate Professor of Pedatrics, North York General Hospital, Toronto, Ontario.

Marlene Bedzow-Weisleder, Speech-Language Pathologist M.S. CCC SLP Reg.CASLPO

Dr Anna Stuckler, PhD, Registered Clinical Psychologist, Toronto, Ontario

Dr. Kurt Andre, Pediatrician, York Central Hospital. Richmond Hill, Ontario

I am truly grateful for all of your time and support.

I would also like to thank all the parents from my clinic who read and provided helpful comments on my book. I appreciate your time and genuine comments. Thank you.

About Dr. Maurice Levy
The Author at a Glance

Dr. Maurice Levy has 35 years of medical experience in hospitals and in his active pediatric primary care and consultation clinic. As the former Chief of Pediatrics and currently, the Head of Research at North York General Hospital in Toronto, Ontario, Dr. Levy has completed numerous degrees and diplomas besides his medical degree in the areas of pediatrics, nephrology, pharmacology, and more. As the leading expert in his field of pediatrics, Dr. Levy has received many awards and published various articles for both health professionals and parents. The following is a brief overview of Dr. Levy's extensive work with children:

- 35 years of medical experience in hospitals & private practice across the globe

- Trained & worked in various prestigious hospitals in Canada, France and Israel (e.g. Hospital for Sick Children, Toronto, Canada)

- Formerly Chief of Pediatrics in the Pediatric Department at North York General Hospital (formerly known as North York Branson Hospital), Toronto, Canada

- Currently Head of Research at North York General Hospital, Toronto, Canada

- Diploma in Pediatric Clinical Pharmacology obtained from The Hospital For Sick Children, Toronto, Canada

- Pediatric Nephrology training at The Hospital For Sick Children, Toronto, Canada

- Research Degree in Clinical Science –University of Montreal, Canada

- Published articles in medical & parenting journals (e.g. "La-Isha", a journal for parents in Israel; "Toronto4Kids"website for parents; "Life for a Baby" Toronto website for parents)

- Formerly member of various committees & associations such as The College of Physicians & Surgeons of Ontario and the Canadian Pediatric Society and many more

- Received various awards & recently awarded the PTPA (Parent-Tested and Parent-Approved) award winner for a book about feeding & nutrition for babies & children, written for parents in 2010

TABLE OF CONTENTS

SECTION 1: DEVELOPMENTAL MILESTONES AND AGES

1 MONTH	2
2 MONTHS	18
3 MONTHS	26
4 MONTHS	35
5 MONTHS	44
6 MONTHS	53
7 MONTHS	65
8 MONTHS	69
9 MONTHS	73
10 MONTHS	83
11 MONTHS	88
12 MONTHS	93
18 MONTHS	106
2 YEARS	115
3 YEARS	129
4 YEARS	142
5 YEARS	155

SECTION 2: IMPORTANT MOTOR DEVELOPMENTAL MILESTONES STAGES

HEAD CONTROL	168
ROLLING OVER	172
SITTING	175
CRAWLING	178
STANDING	182
WALKING	184

SECTION 3: RECOGNITION OF WARNING SIGNS & SYMPTOMS OF DEVELOPMENTAL DISABILITIES

ADHD-ATTENTION DEFICIT HYPERACTIVITY DISORDER	191
AUTISM	198
SPEECH & LANGUAGE DELAY	208
LEARNING DISABILITY	216

SECTION 1:
Developmental Milestones and Ages

Development: 1 Month

1. GENERAL
2. DEVELOPMENTAL MILESTONES
    2.1 PHYSICAL DEVELOPMENT
    2.2 NEWBORN SENSES
    2.3 COGNITIVE & LANGUAGE DEVELOPMENT
    2.4 READING BODY LANGUAGE
    2.5 EMOTIONAL DEVELOPMENT & CRYING
    2.6 GENERAL DEVELOPMENTAL ASPECTS
3. INCREASING NEWBORN DEVELOPMENT & EMOTIONAL SECURITY
4. DEVELOPMENTAL SCREENING & RED FLAGS
5. PARENTAL CONCERNS

1. GENERAL

Congratulations on the arrival of your new baby! You are now ready to learn about what to expect from your newborn in the first month of life. It is important to understand the developmental process, to assess your child's healthy growth and development.

Development is a gradual and exciting process, differing from baby to baby. The first days and weeks of a newborn life is a time of great wonder and progress. Parents play a crucial role at each stage of a baby's growth. It is essential not to compare your baby with others, but to concentrate on each new level of growth. Ensure that you are there for your baby's safety, exploration and learning. *Savor and enjoy every day of the first month of life!*

2. DEVELOPMENTAL MILESTONES

2.1 PHYSICAL DEVELOPMENT

REFLEXES

Reflexes are defined as automatic responses to external (outside) stimulus. Examples of reflexes include yawning, grasping, sucking and so forth.

Most movements are reflexive, as babies' nervous systems are not yet fully developed. As infants grow older, these reflexes will begin to disappear.

During the newborn stage, reflexes will primarily control movement of arms, legs and hands since infants cannot control their body movements. By two months of age, most actions will become voluntary and not reflexive.

The **grasp reflex** is the most common reflex at the newborn age. This is when he closes his hands involuntarily around any object (e.g. fingers) that touches the palm of his hands. The **rooting reflex** is another common reflex, where placing any soft object against your baby's cheek will provoke him to open his mouth and try to suck (a finding food mechanism).

BABY POSITION	DESCRIPTION
HEAD/NECK	<ul><li>Newborns have minimal head control between 1-4 weeks</li><li>The baby's head will wobble uncontrollably and flip backwards (if it is not supported), when placed in a sitting position.</li><li>Baby's head will continue to be unsteady when pulled into a sitting position around one month of age.</li></ul>
ARMS/HANDS/FINGERS	<ul><li>Arms are shaky, jerky and consist of random thrusting.</li><li>Hands and fingers are usually held in a tight fist or slightly opened.</li><li>Fingers are unintentionally able to grasp objects by the grasping reflex.</li><li>Typically, limb movements consist of uncontrolled writhing, meaning that your newborn opens and closes his hands without purpose.</li></ul>
LYING ON THE BACK (SUPINE POSITION)	<ul><li>The newborn may first lie in a flexed and slightly stiff position; yet, the body may follow when his head is turned.</li><li>As the weeks progress in the first month of life, your baby may seem more relaxed in this position.</li></ul>
LYING ON THE STOMACH (PRONE POSITION)	<ul><li>Newborns may turn head from side to side, usually without lifting it from the surface.</li><li>By 4 weeks of age, he can extend his head momentarily while lying on a flat surface.</li></ul>

TIP: Flat Feet

Almost all infants have flat feet. The foot arch may not develop until 4-6 years of age.

2.2 Newborn Senses

There are four main senses newborns are born with. Since the senses are still developing, newborns are especially sensitive to the sights and sounds of other human beings and noises in their environments.

VISION: THROUGH THE EYES OF THE NEWBORN

- Vision is a very important sense in the developing infant, since intellectual development and learning begins with eye contact and visual tracking.
- While your newborn's eyes are physically capable of seeing just fine at birth, his brain is not ready to process all that visual information, so things stay pretty fuzzy for a while. As his brain develops, so does his ability to see clearly, giving him the tools he needs to understand and manage his environment.
- The sense of sight develops gradually over 6-8 months.
- Eye movements are not coordinated in the newborn and the eyes may not begin to move together until 4 weeks or later.
- Within the first month of life, vision undergoes various changes: (see chart on next page)

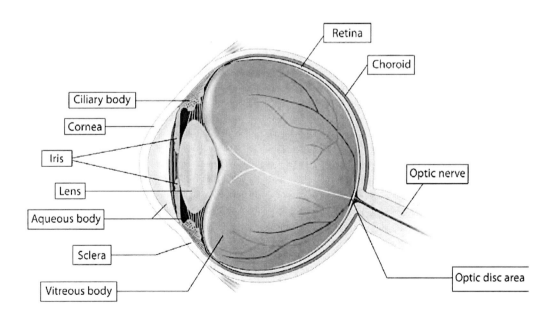

AT BIRTH

- Infants have blurred vision at birth.
- Newborns eyes will most often be closed during the first few days of life, yet some babies keep their eyes open for longer periods.
- Initially, the baby is born with **peripheral vision** (the ability to see to the side). Gradually, he will acquire the ability to focus clearly on a single point in the center of his visual field.
- At first, he cannot focus on anything that is more than 8 to15 inches away (i.e. far enough to identify the person holding him).
- While the baby is able to detect light, shapes and movement, your face is most interesting at this time.

DURING THE 1ST MONTH

Looking at Faces, People and Objects
- Newborns can see parental faces and distinct patterns.
- Objects are seen at a distance of 8 to 15 inches away, with eyes widening and occasionally crossing.

Looking at Lights
- Babies generally focus on light for brief periods of time, but long enough for you to know that they are seeing.
- By the end of the first month, some babies will follow as you move the light slowly towards the center of their field of vision.

Looking at Patterns
- As your baby's retina (the light-sensitive tissue inside the eyeball) develops, his ability to see and recognize patterns improves. The more patterns an object has, the more it will attract your baby's attention.

Color Vision
- The ability to see colors is developing quickly. After only 1 week of life, infants can see the colors red, orange, yellow and green. It does take a little while longer for infants to see blue and violet colors.
- Color vision does not mature until about 4 months of age. For example, the baby cannot know the difference between 2 different colors. However, a red-colored toy is probably preferred over one that is yellow or blue (it is unclear whether this is because of the brightness of the color itself).
- At this point, babies are stimulated more by patterns (e.g. squares, circles) rather than colors. Bold shapes and bold black and white patterns attract babies' attention. They can now see patterns of light and dark.

BY THE END OF THE 1ˢᵀ MONTH

Following Objects
- Your baby will focus briefly on objects as far as 3 feet away, while at the same time, learning to follow or track large moving objects.
- After successfully being able to follow large moving objects, he will begin following small, speedy movements moving from the side to the center of his body.

Recognizing Faces
- The ability to recognize your face or familiar toys in his line of vision is developing and he may become excited by them.

BY 2 MONTHS OF AGE

Looking at People
- Babies will begin to look at people rather than objects and will be able to watch a person directly, follow a moving person with their eyes.

Color Vision
- The brain at this age is improving on distinguishing colors. As such, he may prefer bright primary colors and more detailed or complicated designs.

HEARING

- The sense of hearing is fairly well developed in infants at birth. In fact, it is thought that infants are able to hear sounds in the womb even four months before birth!
- Newborns can hear exaggerated changes in pitches and tones, with a preference for high pitches. They can also recognize certain sounds such as the mother's voice, distinguishable from the male voice.
- Infants are alert to sounds. They recognize sounds by blinking, crying or showing the startle reflex (i.e. arms and legs move away from the body equally).
- Your baby is sensitive to noise levels, so much so that a sudden loud sound may startle him and lead to crying. He may be soothed by consistent, repetitive and soft sounds.
- Babies remember some of the sounds they hear. As such, it is important to repeat reading the same story aloud for several days in a row when your baby is alert and attentive.
- Studies show that infants seem to prefer the sound of the human voice and higher toned (usually female) voices to any other sounds.

It is important for parents to talk to their newborns to stimulate development, even though they cannot understand.

TIP: Newborn Hearing Screen

- The American Academy of Pediatrics (AAP) endorses universal hearing screen tests for newborn infants. This is because hearing loss can go undetected in young children until the preschool years or later.
- Many places will conduct a hearing test in the hospital prior to newborn discharge.
- The tests include the following:
    - OAE = Otoacoustic emissions measure the response to sound by using a small probe inserted in the baby's ear canal. It can be done when the baby is sleeping and causes no discomfort. This test is completed within a few minutes.
    - ABR = Auditory brain stem response uses electrodes placed on the baby's scalp to detect activity in the brain stem's auditory region in response to "clicks" sounded in the baby's ear. It requires the baby to be awake in a quiet state; it is quick and painless.
- If the baby passed the hearing test, then it is unlikely that he has impairments in hearing (though impairments may develop at a later time.)
- If your baby does not pass the initial screening test, it will be repeated to rule out false positive results. Normal screening at birth does not rule out future acquired hearing loss from various medical reasons.
- Discuss concerns with your doctor at any time during your baby's growth if your child:
    1. Does not respond to loud noises.
    2. Does not turn to you when you talk to him (when he reaches 4 months of age).
    3. Does not respond to a sound of a "rattle" type noise when placed close to his ears.
    4. Does not produce a large variety of sounds.

Did You Know

When you are talking with your baby, it is likely that your baby will grow to recognize your voice in the first few days of life and will be soothed by its softness.

TASTE

Newborns are incredibly sensitive to taste stimulation, probably more than they will ever be in their lives. This is made clear with the reactions of babies to sweet, salty and bitter tastes. Often times, bitter or sour tastes provoke crying or funny faces.

Babies tend to have a sweet tooth since breast milk and formula have very sweet tastes.

SMELL

Newborns are present with the sense of smell at birth. They can use the sense of smell to recognize the caregiver. Moreover, they are able to identify objects by smelling or tasting them.

2.3 Cognitive & Language Development

- **At birth**, the only way infants can communicate is by **crying**. Initially, it is a reflexive behavior, beginning to disappear within the first month.
- **By one month of age**, infants will watch their mothers while they are talking and if their focus is close enough, infants will **mimic speaking** by opening and closing their mouths. In addition, infants will imitate movements of their mother's face.
- **Between 1-2 months of age**, babies will start making gurgling and cooing noises as a mark of pleasure and contentment. At this age, they may begin to grunt and sigh as well.

Distinguishing sounds:
- Newborn infants can distinguish **their mother's voice** from all other adults. Upon hearing her voice, the infant's eyes will move towards that direction.
- When she is less than twelve inches away, infants will try to follow the mother's face with the eyes.
- The baby is increasingly able **to recognize family voices** and make small "throaty" noises.
- The **first voluntary smile** is being noticed, though it is usually not seen until 2-3 months of age; it is the earliest sign of mental growth.

2.4 Reading Baby Body Language

- Watching what your baby does and how he responds will help you understand his body language.
- Babies certainly have their own way of telling you what is going on. It is mostly done through various styles of crying (initially), smiling (couple of months) and incomprehensible chatter (around 5 months of age).
- Alert babies are more interested in communication when using a lot of facial expressions. This way, your baby can watch what you are doing and slowly get used to the idea that you are both communicating.
- Noises are attempts to gain your attention such as vowel sounds.

2.5 Emotional Development & Crying

Crying is one of the first ways infants communicate. "I talk by crying" could mean such things as: "I am wet; I am too cold or too hot; I want to change positions; I want to be held; I need to be burped; I am sleepy; I am hungry; I have colic; I am sick". As time progresses, you will be able to eventually differentiate between each cry and know what your baby is crying out for.

TIP: Crying & Comforting
Many babies stop crying when their mother picks them up, because they know (through their senses) that their mother is a source of comfort.

2.6 General Developmental Aspects
SLEEP
- Babies should always sleep on their back at the young age of one month.
- Most babies will sleep through the night by 3-4 months of age, but lucky parents can get a good night's sleep sooner!
- Your baby needs encouragement to sleep throughout the night. Place him in bed when he is drowsy, but slightly awake. Avoid rocking him to sleep or holding him until he falls asleep since he needs to learn to fall asleep on his own.
- Try to ignore your baby's squirms or whimpering; try to let him fall asleep on his own.

> **PARENT WATCH: SIDS (Sudden Infant Death Syndrome) & Sleep**: Many SIDS experts believe that nothing should be in the baby's crib other than the baby! Often, parents place bumpers in the crib to protect the baby's head and limbs. However, bumpers may be dangerous, because it can cause suffocation and the same is true for any soft or fluffy item (e.g. pillow, toys) in the crib. The SIDS Alliance (a parental organization) does not object to bumpers that are thin and firm.
> **Comment on wedges**: The American Academy of Pediatrics (AAP) does not endorse Wedges used to keep babies on their side, since no studies have proven their effectiveness or safety.

FEEDING
- Babies love the parental bonding that occurs during feeding sessions. The affection and touching received during feeding is an important part of the infant diet.
- Feed your newborn breast milk and/or iron-fortified formula.
- Do not use the microwave to heat formula.

3. INCREASING NEWBORN DEVELOPMENT AND EMOTIONAL SECURITY

It is never too early to start to stimulate development, even though most of newborn behavior is dominated by reflex and instincts. Consider the following to foster your newborn's emotional security and newborn development:

- ✓ **Hold** him face-to-face.
- ✓ **Talk** in a soothing tone and allow him to hear your affectionate voice.
- ✓ **Sing** to your baby.
- ✓ Walk with your baby in a sling, carrier or stroller and talk to him as you go.
- ✓ **Rock** him in a rhythmic and gentle motion.
- ✓ **Respond quickly** to your baby's cries to let him know that you are there when he needs you. Parents cannot always console babies. Though, they can always **check to see** that the baby is comfortable, not too hot or cold, hungry or wet.

- ✓ Do not worry about spoiling your baby.
- ✓ The **best toys** to use for this age group include toys that move, are curvy and have high contrast that are easy for baby to see such as pictures of faces or toys with faces (ideal toys), mobiles (place a black & white mobile above his cot), etc.
- ✓ **Change** your baby's position once in a while.
- ✓ **Encourage** all family members to help care for the infant.
- ✓ Remember that a lot of your infant's development depends on interactions between the two of you.

Newborn Behaviors

Some findings in newborns that concern parents are not actual signs of illness. Most of these are harmless reflexes and are due to an immature nervous system. These often disappear by 2-3 months of age and include chin trembling, lower lip quivering, and noise from nose breathing.

4. DEVELOPMENTAL SCREENING AND RED FLAGS

It is important to review and repeat developmental screenings at every age of your child's life in order to assess progression, regression, or any difficulties. Developmental skills are to be mastered by the appropriate age in about 85-90% of children. Review the following developmental screening to assess your child's development. If you check one or more "no" responses or a *red flag* is present, then discuss with your child's health professional.

PHYSICAL DEVELOPMENT

- Slightly lifts head when lying on the stomach and moves head side to side
- Lifts head for short periods in the prone position
- Symmetrical jerky arm and leg movements

YES	NO

VISION

- Prefers the human face to other shapes
- Focuses longer on a face when spoken to
- Focuses on objects 8-15 inches away (especially your face)
- Focuses eyes to a short distance

YES	NO

COGNITIVE DEVELOPMENT

- Stops sucking when distracted
- Quiet in response to touch
- Cries for assistance
- Able to distinguish mother's voice from those of others
- Tries to mimic speaking by opening and closing the mouth

YES	NO

HEARING

- Responds to loud and sudden noises by startling, crying, or quieting
- Alert to sounds

YES	NO

For the following "Definite Red Flags", please contact your child heath professional if any one of your answers is "yes".

DEFINITE RED FLAGS
- Poor sucking and slow feeding
- Legs or arms seem stiff without much movement or floppy
- Not lifting head much when lying on stomach after first few weeks
- Does not blink when shown a bright light
- Does not follow a nearby object moving side to side or does not look at you
- Does not respond to loud sounds or sudden noises
- One of the pupils is different from the other (e.g. white)

YES	NO

5. PARENTAL CONCERNS

How can I tell if my newborn can see?
- Most newborns can see small objects by 3-4 months of age and color by 5-6 months. By 1 year of age, a child will reach full normal adult vision.
- Consult your child's health professional when:
  - He is unable to make steady eye contact by 2-3 months of age
  - He is unable to focus on objects
  - There is constant crossed eyes or one eye turns out (most babies have occasional crossed eyes in the first three months)
  - He is unable to track objects with eyes as the object moves across his field of vision by 3 months of age
  - The pupils appears whiter/bigger or of different size
  - The eyes flutter quickly from side to side or up and down

Are crossed eyes in a newborn normal?
- Many infants present with intermittent/occasional short episodes of crossed eyes in the first 1-3 months of life. As such, crossed eyes in a newborn are mostly normal.
- If your baby's eyes cross inward or outward or do not appear to focus together, then strabismus may be to blame. Strabismus is a misalignment of the eyes resulting from eye muscles failing to work together.
- Consult your child's health professional especially if there is family history of strabismus (cross eyed):
  - ✓ Episodes do not disappear by 4 months of age
  - ✓ Deviation is frequent or persistent and especially if it is the same eye
  - ✓ Possibility of true crossed eyes (i.e. strabismus) where the baby only uses one eye to follow objects while the other seems to be looking elsewhere.

- Early treatment of strabismus is important, because much of what a child learns is learned through his eyes. Ignoring crossed eyes can lead to "lazy eye" where the eye becomes weaker through disuse.

Why does my newborn cry without tears?
- Tears are produced by the lachrymal system located under the upper eyelid. It develops in the first three years of life.
- Although newborns are physiologically able to produce tears, they mostly cry without them. The reason for this is unclear.
- Some interesting facts about new born tears:
    - ✓ The neural wiring in a newborn is immature and does not yet have the emotional intensity necessary to produce tears.
    - ✓ Babies are born with basal tearing, which means that their tear ducts deliver just enough "wet stuff" to keep the eye moist and healthy. Newborns do not have tearing that indicates emotional distress just yet.
    - ✓ If tear production is not fully developed, some babies may not shed tears for many months, until there is enough moisture to coat the surface of their eyes.
    - ✓ It is usually between 2-4 months of age that a baby's emotional tears kick in. Triggers for tears may include frustration, loneliness, pain, tiredness and so forth. These triggers may cause the nervous system to stimulate a nerve in the brain that sends a message to the tear ducts.
    - ✓ Dehydration can affect tear production, especially when infants and children are significantly dehydrated.
    - ✓ In rare conditions, infants and children may not produce tears (familial dysautonomia, ectodermal dysplasia, congenital sjogren's syndrome, All-groove syndrome, and so forth).

Blocked Tear Ducts – My baby's eyes are always watery. What does this mean?
- The role of the lachrymal glands system is to produce tears to keep the eye moist. Typically, tears drain through small holes located in the inner part of the eye near the nose. The tears flow from the nasal-lachrymal duct and some of it is stored in a structure called: nasal-lachrymal sac.
- In infants, the nasal-lachrymal duct is not yet fully mature and developed, causing the duct to be narrower.
- If your baby's eye is continuously watery, then your baby may have blocked tear duct(s). This means that the channel that normally carries tears from the eye to the nose is blocked or not fully matured.
- Blocked tear ducts is a common condition with more than 90% opening at 6-12 months of age.
- It can affect one or more eyes.

What To Do About Blocked Tear Ducts
- Keep your baby's eyes clean by using a warm, moist and clean cotton ball or washcloth to gently wipe the eye whenever you see discharge.
- If your baby awakens with a crusty crating that prevents an eye from opening, then hold a clean, warm and wet compress over the eyes to loosen the crust. Then, wipe it away with a fresh cotton ball or cloth.
- Gently massage the tear duct in the inner corner of the eye (A little sac where tears accumulate is located in the inner lower corner of the eye). Wash your hands and place your finger along the side of your baby's nose. Apply slight pressure while pressing down toward the corner of the nose. Massage inward towards the nose for a minute or so and repeat several times throughout the day.
- Sometimes, your child's pediatrician may prescribe antibiotic eye drops or ointments to resolve any eye infections. However, most cases are resolved on their own.

When to See the Doctor About Blocked Tear Ducts
Consult your child's health professional when:
- The eyelids are red or swollen
- The whites of your baby's eye look red
- Red lumps appear at the inner lower corner of the eyelids
- Eye is still watery at 12 months of age
- You have questions and concerns

TIP: Tears Production - From birth to 1 month of age

Although the obstruction is present at birth, the delay of onset of symptoms can be explained by the occasional delay in tear production until the age of 3-4 weeks in some babies.

When I take pictures of my baby, will the flash affect his eyes?
- No, the flash will not affect your baby's eyes even when taken at a close distance.
- The fact that your child blinks when a picture is taken means that he has a normal reflex for vision.

Bow legs in my baby?
- The legs of most babies are always bowed at birth from being wrapped tightly around their bodies inside the mother's womb. This bowing is normal and persists until about 18-24 months of age.
- There is no danger that standing will bow your baby's legs.
- This is a myth that originated from when babies have rickets and vitamin D deficiency that caused bone softening and bowing of the legs.
- **Caution**: If the bowing is extreme and does not improve by 18-24 months of age, then consult your child's health professional.

GOOD TO KNOW: Never Ever Shake Your Baby!
<ul><li>Some parents shake the baby to stop him from crying or during play.</li><li>Any child can die from being shaken, regardless of their age. However, children under the age of two years and infants who are unable to hold their head up are most vulnerable.</li><li>Never shake your baby during play or out of anger.</li><li>If you experience uncontrollable anger, do not use physical abuse; get help for yourself.</li><li>Always provide support for a baby's head when holding, playing or transporting him.</li><li>Notify family members and caregivers about proper head support and the risks of shaking a young infant or child.</li><li>Most cases of shaken babies occur when the baby does not stop crying. Try to allow others to help you if you are tired and frustrated with your little one. If you have to, leave the room for a few minutes until you relax while taking deep breaths.</li><li>It is better to take time out for yourself by allowing your baby to cry and removing yourself from the situation that can cause any potential damage to the baby.</li></ul>

Eye Color: Can 2 brown-eyed parents have a blue-eyed baby?
- It is very common for two parents with similar eye colors to have a baby with an entirely different color.
- It is possible for a child with a different eye color than the parents to share this color with an ancestor in the family.
- Blue eyes in the first few months of life can become green, hazel or brown (depending on the level of melanin – brown pigments the iris contains) or eyes can stay blue (if there is little melanin pigments). Brown eyes wont ever turn blue, since eyes don't lose melanin once it is there.
- Eye color usually retains a permanent color by the age of 6 months.

What can I do to stimulate vision at birth or by 3 months?
At birth, you can:
- Give your baby lots of face time by playing with him/her, talking and making lots of expressions and noises that your baby seems to enjoy.
- Hold bold black and white patterns that your child can see.
- Bright lights may be irritating to the newborn eye, so ensure that you dim the lights.

By 3 months, you can:
- Try raising your eyebrows or puckering your lips and wait for your baby to respond.
- Babies like to mimic facial expressions, so make as many as you can for your baby to imitate.
- Pairs of bold and contrasting colors are easiest for the young baby to see. At this age, he sees red, orange and green best.
- Let the baby hang out with the family to encourage visual stimulation.

Development: 2 Months

1. GENERAL

2. DEVELOPMENTAL MILESTONES

2.1 PHYSICAL

2.2 VISION & HEARING

2.3 SOCIO-EMOTIONAL & LANGUAGE

2.4 SPEECH & LANGUAGE

2.5 GENERAL DEVELOPMENTAL ASPECTS

3. PARENTING & STIMULATING THE TWO-MONTH-OLD

4. DEVELOPMENTAL SUMMARY

5. RED FLAGS

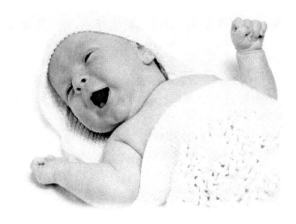

1. GENERAL

By the second month, your baby has settled into a fairly stable routine. He will lose the newborn reflexes and acquire more voluntary control of the body. Generally, newborn reflexes begin to disappear around six weeks of age, as your baby progresses from being unresponsive and quiet to being more active and alert.

2. DEVELOPMENTAL MILESTONES

2.1 Physical Development

HEAD/ NECK
- He may be able to turn his head from side to side.
- Rather than being able to turn his head, he begins to look around with his eyes when he hears an interesting sound.
- The head can now be raised slightly further when lying on the tummy and when held over the shoulder.
- When in a car seat or carrier, your baby can slightly raise his head, especially if he has a lot of support and you provide special head rests designed to help him in these situations.

ARMS/ HANDS/ LEGS
- Movements are less jerky, progressing to more circular and smooth motions
- Able to hold onto objects for a few moments, sometimes longer (the grasping reflex is being replaced with a more controlled response)
- Closed fists are now more open and will readily grasp a rattle if you gently lay one close to the palm of the hand
- He can play with his hands and press his palms together
- Able to hold a toy in his fist, but cannot yet look at it as he does so (he has yet to make the connection between the toy he is holding and what he is doing with his hands)
- Arms move around randomly but quite energetically
- May now suck his thumb or finger
- Explores extremities (hands and feet)

TIP: Head Lifting and Leg Straightening

Between now and four months of age, most babies will start to lift their head, neck and upper chest on their forearm, craning their necks like a turtle to see what is going on around them. They will also straighten out their legs when you let them sit on your lap and try to stand with support – this will not cause them to be bowlegged.

2.2 Vision and Hearing

Your baby's **eyes are more coordinated** and can work together to move and focus at the same time. Soon, he will be able to track an object (fixed look at an object 15-30 cm away from him), and move through an entire half circle in front of him. Your baby **may follow objects and movements** at 180 degrees initially, from one side to the other and then from up to down and later, even in circles. He will start noticing small objects (e.g. a small, shiny button or raisin) that may attract his attention and he may follow objects of interest such as those objects with sharp, intense color. This increased visual coordination will provide him with the depth perception he needs to track objects as they move toward and away from him.

At about two months of age, you may begin hearing your infant repeat some vowel sounds (ah-ah-ah, ooh-ooh-ooh), especially if you have been talking to him often with clear, simple words and phrases. He will respond to loud sounds by becoming completely silent, crying or acting startled. **Hearing is becoming more directed** and he may stop his activity to listen to a new sound.

2.3 Socio-Emotional & Language Development

The following are socio-emotional developments of the two-month-old child. This is how your child begins to relate to other people and how he feels about himself and interacting with others.

- Smiles upon social contact
- Listens to voices and cues and may even respond
- Alert for longer hours of the day
- Able to demonstrate satisfaction
- Pleasure is shown when interacting with parents
- Increased interest in the outside world

> **Babies Temperaments?**
> Remember that all babies are unique and they each have different temperaments. Many are quiet and calm, while others are very active and some are very sensitive and fuss easily. Some may even need less stimulating environments to stay calm than others. Try to keep your baby's temperament in check as you react to his needs.

SMILING
True social smiling does not start until about 6-7 weeks of age. With the first real smile, your baby will use his whole face and not just his mouth. Babies will smile earlier if they are spoken to, played with and cuddled a lot. Some babies smile as they are falling asleep, urinating or as their cheeks are stroke. It may be a sign of comfort or contentment.

2.4 Speech & Language

Developments in communication and language in your infant include:

- Smiling and crying are your baby's principal means of communication
- While crying alerts you to all kinds of problems, smiling may be interpreted as appreciation and recognition for your efforts and attention
- May giggle or coo in response to your conversation with him
- Startled by loud sounds
- By 6 weeks, your baby will turn to sounds and begin to watch your face when you talk and smile
- Touch is an important means of communication with your baby

2.5 General Developmental Aspects

FEEDING
- "Spitting up" is common; as long as your baby is thriving, it is a nuisance, rather than a problem
- Breastfeeding and/or formula are still provided at this age

SLEEP
- Always put your baby to sleep on his back
- Alternate the end of the crib when you place his head so that he does not always sleep with his head on one side
- Begin to establish a bedtime routine to discourage night awakening

- Infants sleep most of the day but a child's sleep patterns vary from baby to baby
- Many babies will sleep through the night by 3 months and "lucky" parents get good night sleep sooner
- A quiet baby is may simply be not tired enough to go to sleep for a long time

3. PARENTING & STIMULATING THE TWO- MONTH OLD

Your baby is happy to see people, yet does not demand a lot of attention nor can he get up and crawl around to get things. He may become responsive when you talk to him and he is beginning to blossom into a "real" person. Continue to hold, rock, cradle, sing, and talk to your baby as much as possible. Every interaction with your baby stimulates brain development. By responding quickly and enthusiastically to your baby's smiles and engaging with him often in "conversation", you will let your child know that he is important to you and that he can trust you. Also, by recognizing and looking at him while he is talking, you will show him that you are interested in what he has to say and that you value him.

Encourage your baby to "speak" by talking with him during dressing, bathing, feeding, playing, walking and driving. Use appropriately aged toys to stimulate your baby such as rattles, mobiles or other objects so that your infant can begin to reach for objects and watch them.

As parents, you should continue to have adequate rest, fresh air (e.g. going for walks). Continue providing your child with extra head support until his neck muscles get stronger.

TIP: Toys Suggestions
Ensure toys are always too big to fit in his mouth; e.g. Teething ring, rattle, toys that make noise, soft toys without detachable parts (See chapter on toys)

Your baby may respond by cooing or giggling even more when you stimulate his senses. Remember that babies prefer more complex designs, colors and shapes so allow your baby to constantly touch and look at various objects or people. You can help stimulate your baby's senses by doing the following:

- Add colors (e.g. brightly colored mobile in the crib)
- Play music to stimulate sensory development. Hum or sing when you are close by.

- Pay attention (watching your baby to see what he considered attractive and frightening; e.g. try different tones of voice and songs)
- Cuddle (babies need loving attention)
- Hold your baby close so that he can study your face
- Respond to your baby's cries, though not always; he will learn that you are there when hungry, tired, cold, needs new diaper, discomforted and so forth. To help him relax, hold, cuddle, rock, sing or talk to your baby
- Carry your baby around and show him *various shapes, colors and lights*
- Make conversation with your baby whenever you have the chance, but particularly when he makes noises, utters sounds, and looks your way
- Talk about everyday things as you normally do
- Share a book, ideally with simple black and white pictures initially
- Rattles are a great toy; as the rattle is waved in your baby's hands, he will hear the noise and begin to make the connection between the rattle and his moving it – learning that if you can hear something, you can probably see it too
- Sound-source locating sounds that are out of sight will help extend your baby's field of exploration and this is an important skill to develop
- The baby gym is great since he can lie on his back and focus on the brightly colored shapes
- Playing with him, moving him to a new location several times a day and often changing his position

> **TIP: Pacifier Use**
> If using a pacifier, try and restrict its use when your baby seems to need the self-comforting behavior of sucking. Avoid using it every time your baby cries. It is usually better to pick up and hold your baby to comfort him when he is crying.

5. DEVELOPMENTAL SUMMARY

Your baby *should* be able to:
- Smile in response to your smile
- Follow an object in an arc of 15 cm above the face to the midline
- Respond to a bell in some way (startled, crying, quieting)
- Vocalize in a way other than crying (e.g. cooing)

Your baby will *probably* be able to:
- Lift his head when lying on the tummy
- Follow an object in an arc about 15 cm above the face, past the midline (straight ahead)

Your baby *may possibly* be able to:
- Bring both hands together
- When lying on the stomach, lift his head 90 degrees
- Follow an object in an arc about 15 cm above the face for 180 degrees and from one side to the other

Your baby *may even* be able to:
- Hold his head steady when upright
- When lying on the stomach, raise his chest, supported by the arm
- Roll over one way
- Grasp a rattle holder by the tips of his fingers
- Pay attention to noises or other small objects
- Say "ah-goo" or smaller vowel-consonant combinations

5. RED FLAGS

Consult your child's health professional should your child *not* display any of the following red flags:

- Respond to loud sounds
- Smiles at the sound of your voice by two months of age
- Follows moving objects by 2-3 months of age
- Smile at people by 3 months of age
- Improvement in head control or show extreme floppiness
- Lift the head when faced down
- Focuses on caregivers eyes
- Moves both arms and legs actively in play when in a supine position
- Use eyes to follow or focus on an adult face
- Shows maternal infant interaction
- Enjoys being touched or cuddled

6. PARENT CONCERN

Is it normal for my baby to sleep with his eyes open?

General
- Sleeping with the eyes open is fairly common in infants. Although most outgrow it by 12-18 months.
- While sleeping with the eyes open certainly looks odd, it is usually normal and does not indicate that your child has a sleep problem
- There is some evidence to suggest that sleeping with open eye is hereditary

Causes
- Causes for sleeping with open eyes are unknown
- It may be associated with a baby spending more time in REM (Rapid Eye Movement) sleep, which is a more active sleep cycle. Newborn infants spend more time in REM sleep than adults, which may cause open eyes during sleep. (Common in REM sleep)
- It is very rare that a malformation of the eyelids, facial nerve damage or certain types of tumors prevent the child from closing his eyes normally.

What to do & When to Seek Help
- You can gently stroke your child's eyelids closed if the open eyes really scares or bothers you.
- If your baby sleeps with his eyes open for many hours at a time or if he does it regularly after he age of 18 months, then you should consult you health professional

Development: 3 Months

1. GENERAL

2. DEVELOPMENTAL MILESTONES

2.1 PHYSICAL DEVELOPMENT

2.2 VISION

2.3 HEARING, SPEECH & LANGUAGE

2.4 COGNITIVE DEVELOPMENT

2.5 SOCIO-EMOTIONAL DEVELOPMENT

3. ENHANCING DEVELOPMENT

4. DEVELOPMENTAL SCREENING & RED FLAGS

1. GENERAL

At the age of three months, primitive reflexes continue to disappear, indicating a shift from reflex behavior to willed muscular control. Smoother and more purposeful motions replace these reflexes. Your baby's specific personality type will be the result of her genetics combined with her environment. You will begin to recognize different types of cries and their related needs and you finally find a little predictability with your little one. Sleeping, eating and alertness patterns will become more regular.

In respect to sleeping, many babies cry before they sleep. This type of cry relieves them of stress and allows them to go from a waking state to a sleeping one. Also, sleep patterns may begin to settle down at this age, providing you with some rest with many 3-4 month old babies sleeping well for a good six-hour stretch.

2. DEVELOPMENTAL MILESTONES
2.1 PHYSICAL DEVELOPMENT

HEAD AND NECK
- Head and eye control improves and the head wobbling decreases when the head is in an upright position. It is held steady for several seconds before bobbing forward again
- When lying on her back, she can raise her head several inches high and hold it for a while. Lying on her stomach, she can lift her head up to a 45-90 degree angle.
- Follow a dangling ball 6-12 inches away from face
- By the end of 3 months, she is able to turn her head to the left and right and follow adult movements within available visual fields.

BODY
- Can roll over one way.
- Able to sit with back rounded in a tripod position with support. The head lag is partially compensated.
- In the prone position (lying on the stomach), she can lift her chest and head up for a second, using her forearm for support. She can also lean on her elbow while in this position.

HANDS

- Can hold a rattle for a moment when it is placed in her hands.
- The hands are becoming an important point of vision. She spends a lot of time "watching" her fingers and hands. She can also bring both hands together into the middle over the chest or chin.
- Her fingers may be open half of the time instead of always clenched up. She is beginning to clasp and unclasp.
- Gradually, she will be able to reach her mouth with her hands and may begin sucking on a finger(s). This is a big step, as she associated this action with results.
- Actions become more voluntary, with the baby trying to reach for objects with her hands, grasp it and hold it for a few moments.

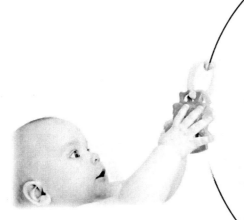

ARMS AND LEGS

- She has better hand, arm and leg coordination
- She is able to move or lift her hands to the side and bring them to the center
- Trying and reaching for objects is a constant endeavor. Often, she is able to hold a toy and lift it voluntarily
- Limb movement is more pliable and smooth with vigorous kicks; legs alternating or occasionally together. She may even be able to bear some weight on her legs when held upright

2.2 VISION

- There is greater control of eye movements due to increased cortical development.
- Visually, the 3-month-old is very alert. She is gaining control over her eyes, making it more likely for her to make eye contact with others.
- She searches out the source of sounds with her eye
- She can converge the eye when a dangling ball is moved towards her face.
- Color is becoming important at this age as she enjoys bright and vibrant colors.
- A defensive blank is clearly shown
- Recognizes a feeding bottle and is eagerly excited as the bottle approaches.
- Watching faces intensely is a hallmark at this age.

2.3 Hearing, Speech & Language

- May turn eyes and/or head towards the source of a sound, following a moving object with the eyes
- Relaxed when listening to voices or music (sometimes she will even try to answer these voices)
- Begins practicing sounds particularly in the morning
- Quiet or smiling to the mother's voice (recognizes your voice); quiet to the sound of a rattle or spoon in a cup or a small ringing bell for 3-5 seconds
- Sudden loud noises still disturb her, provoking blinking, eye twitching, crying and turning over
- Begins to babble

2.4 Cognitive Development
(Thinking, Learning & Memory)

- Shows interest in objects; enjoys touching them (likes shape, color, texture)
- Learns that there are various stages of textures, as well as warm/cold
- Learns that some objects change their shape when touched. Enjoys watching objects return to a normal shape when released

- A new awareness for hands; it is part of the body (hands are one of the first objects your baby will grasp)
- When a toy falls, the baby believes it has disappeared and will not attempt looking for it with her hands or eyes
- Begins identifying family members and discerns between them; distinctively begins to prefer some people over others; likely to still smile at strangers, especially when the stranger looks the baby straight in the eyes and coos or talks to her
- Often sucks or licks lips in response to sounds of preparation for feeding

TIP: Parental Verbal Stimulation & Child Intelligence

Recent research indicates that higher intelligence is associated with how many words a child hears in the first year of life. As such, verbal stimulation is incredibly important. If you are bilingual, your child will benefit from hearing both languages being regularly spoken. Have fun and let each parent speak to the baby in a different language!

2.5 Socio-Emotional Development

By three months of age, your baby will be a master of "smile talking". The whole body will be engaged in the sort of talk that begins and ends with a smile with the hands opening wide, arms lifting upwards and legs moving in tune with the rhythms of your speech. Your baby will:

- Sustains social contact
- Begins reacting to situations by cooing or showing excited movements (e.g. when about to take a bath or feeding)
- Responds with smiles and obvious pleasure to friendly voices and familiar faces
- Smiles spontaneously & voluntarily; squeals & gargles when happy
- Enjoys being kissed & hurled on the stomach
- Protests when left alone for a long time
- Cries when uncomfortable & annoyed
- Enjoys interaction with others, especially the mother/primary caregiver
- Attempts to gain the parent's attention when they are close
- The combination of movements & colors of toys can be fascinating
- May stop sucking her thumb/bottle to listen to your voice
- Becoming more animated & engaging with flashing smiles & cooing

TIP: When Baby's Cry and Spoiling

Most experts recommend soothing a baby's cries as soon as possible for at least the first few months of life. It is virtually impossible to spoil your new infant so hold and swing her continuously. As your baby grows and you see how capable she is to entertain herself, she can also use those same skills to calm herself down when a crying spell occurs. If she is unable to calm herself down, use toys, books or music to comfort her rather than picking her up all the time.

3. ENHANCING DEVELOPMENT

a) Hold a toy at an attractable **distance from your baby and watch for the waving of her arms.** Now move the object away so that **she can possibly reach for it (learning depth perception).**

b) To encourage her to follow a moving object and **to stimulate her visual perception,** have her do the following: (a) you sit or lie on the floor facing your baby at eye level; (b) bring your head close to the baby and move it from side to side, saying "look at mommy" and see if your baby's eyes are following your face; and (c) you may use a puppet or a doll and move it in front of your baby, making sure that she cannot see your face.

c) **Alternate her body** between lying on the back and stomach so that she knows that there are other options.

d) **Use dangling objects and bright colored toys** that move or make sounds. **Place them within reach of your baby's arms and legs.** This will teach her the impact of **cause and effect.**

e) **Encourage hand development** by placing toys close to your baby and see if she will **reach to grasp them.**

f) **Read and sing** to your baby and use her name in the songs. Reading to your child, even at such a young age, as well as, letting her hear you read helps your baby develop an ear for the cadence of language. **Varying the pitch of your voice,** using accents, singing and vocalizing makes the connection between you and your baby that much more stimulating.

g) **Have a conversation** with her and stop to "listen", pause for responding and so forth. This will teach her the art of conversation.

h) As you dress your baby, **tell her what you are doing** and name the body parts.

i) Gently clap your baby's hands together, bending her arms and legs.

j) **Play with her,** showing her new things, as she wants your attention.

k) **Hang toys and mobiles** on either side of the crib – keep in mind it must be low and in the line of vision.

l) **Stimulate her sense of touch** with a variety of materials (e.g. fur, tissue, felt and terry cloth).

m) **Massage and kiss her** on the nose and so forth as a way of relaxation and engaging your baby.

n) **Listening and observation** help babies learn.

4. DEVELOPMENTAL SCREENING AND RED FLAGS

Fill out the following questionnaire to assess your child's 3-month-old developmental patterns. If one or more "no" answers are checked off, then consult your child's health professional regarding any questions and/or concerns. Note that some aspects may need training experience and therefore, may not be developed when not yet attempted.

PHYSICAL DEVELOPMENT

	YES	NO

Gross Motor Skills:
- Supports her head well
- Lies on back, lifts her head up to at least 5 degrees
- Prone position (lies on stomach) lifts head and chest for a second using support

Fine Motor Skills:
- Grasps and holds objects
- Able to move and bring arms to the side and to the center

LANGUAGE, SPEECH AND HEARING

Receptive Skills:

Turns to you when you speak

Smiles upon hearing your voice

Jumps upon hearing loud voices

Stops activities and attends closely to unfamiliar sounds

Turns to where a sound is coming from

Expressive Skills:

Coos when content

Takes turns cooing in response to other cooing

Randomly babbles

Smiles at you when you come into view

Uses different cries for different needs

YES	NO

YES	NO

COGNITIVE DEVELOPMENT

Begins identifying family members (distinctly begins to prefer some people over others)

Learns that some objects change their shape when touched

Enjoys watching objects return to their original shapes after being changed when touched

Shows interest in objects and enjoy playing with them

YES	NO

SOCIO-EMOTIONAL DEVELOPMENT

Sustains social contact

Reacts to situations by cooing or showing excited movements

Responds with smiles and obvious pleasure to friendly voices and familiar people

Enjoys interactions with others, especially the mother

YES	NO

VISION	YES	NO
Follows moving objects with her eyes in an arc about 15 cm above the face past the midline		
Makes eye contact with you by the end of 3 months of age		
Watches or follows an object with the eye by the end of 3 months of age		

For the following "Definite Red Flags", contact your child health professional if any one of your answers is "yes".

DEFINITE RED FLAGS

If one or more "yes" answers are checked off, then consult your child's health professional.

	YES	NO
Lack of coordinated eye movements		
Drifting of one eye when looking at objects		
Turning or tilting of the head when looking at objects		
Frequent "wiggling, drifting, jerking" of the eye		
Rolling at less than 3 months of age*		
Persistent Fisting**		
Lack of social smiling***		

NOTE:
* Indicative of Hypertonia: increased muscle tone
** Indicative of Neuron-motor dysfunction: dysfunction of the nervous system
*** Indicative of Visual Difficulties, Attachment problems, and/or Cognitive Delays

Development: 4 Months

1. GENERAL

2. DEVELOPMENTAL MILESTONES

2.1 PHYSICAL DEVELOPMENT: GROSS MOTOR SKILLS

2.2 PHYSICAL DEVELOPMENT: FINE MOTOR SKILLS

2.3 VISION

2.4 LANGUAGE & HEARING

2.5 SOCIO-EMOTIONAL DEVELOPMENT

2.6 COGNITIVE DEVELOPMENT

2.7 ADDITIONAL DEVELOPMENTAL ASPECTS

3. ENHANCING DEVELOPMENT

4. DEVELOPMENTAL SCREENING & RED FLAGS

1. GENERAL

At four months of age, the baby is developing external features. For example, baby's hair may start changing in color and texture, eye color will be more pronounced, muscles are developing and strengthening, and more generally, the four month old is turning into a beautiful young baby. At four months of age, infants are described as "hatching" socially. They are becoming increasingly interested in the wider world. During feeding, infants no longer focus exclusively on the mother, but become distracted in the mothers arms, preferring to face outwards.

2. DEVELOPMENTAL MILESTONES

2.1 PHYSICAL DEVELOPMENT: GROSS MOTOR SKILLS

Gross motor skills are the abilities acquired throughout the lifespan involving large muscle groups and whole body movements such as standing, walking, running, etc.
The following table outlines the gross motor skills developed at four months of age:

HEAD	TRUNK	LEGS
<ul><li>Moves head in all directions</li><li>Able to turn head to any side while lying or sitting</li><li>Holds head straight up for a short period of time</li><li>Lying on the stomach, your baby is able to lift head and hold it in a 90 degree angle</li><li>Lifts head when lying on back with chin touching chest</li><li>Supine position: able to reach and grasp objects and bring them to mouth</li></ul>	<ul><li>Sitting position: no head lag when pulling up to a sitting position; baby begins turning from his stomach onto his back (the reverse is developed at a later stage); most babies are able to complete this turn by the end of the 4th month</li><li>Back still requires support when sitting, but his head is able to hold up better</li></ul>	<ul><li>Imitates movements of swimming</li><li>Able to advance in the crib</li><li>Plays with legs in the bath</li><li>Able to bear weight on the legs</li><li>Able to stand up with help</li><li>When bringing your child from a sitting to standing position, he will help by pushing his legs</li></ul>

2.2 Physical Development: Fine Motor Skills & Vision

Fine motor skills include those abilities that involve the refined use of small muscle movements (e.g. picking up objects), the pincer grasp (holding an object between the thumb and forefinger), etc.

HAND/FINGER COORDINATION

- Beginning to **use fingers separately** rather than using the entire hand. The more delicate workings of each finger are being used as sophisticated skills develop. For example, your baby may enjoy scratching at this age.
- Able to **hold objects briefly** when placed in his hands.
- **Pull objects closer to his mouth** and **holds small toys between his thumbs and fingers**.
- **Reaching out** for objects becomes a developmental mark at this stage, even though he may often miss the object.
- At this stage, he could be able to pick up objects with either hand and transfer it into the other hand, completing **back and forth actions**.

MORE TO KNOW: Hand Use
Since your baby is unable to walk or crawl yet, he is trying to pull the world towards him. He studies his hands and at some point, he will stuff them into his mouth. Once a baby masters these skills, he will try more tricky things (e.g. grabbing one hand with the other and then pulling them apart).

2.3 Vision

- Glances from one object to another
- **Coordination between baby's eyes and hands** is improving (e.g. if he sees a toy, he will motion his hands for it).
- **Focus is fixed for a longer period of time,** despite the fact that he prefers to look at closer objects. By the end of fourth months, he will be able to focus on objects, whether they are close or far in distance.
- A major breakthrough: he is able to **see color**! While babies see color from birth, they have extreme difficulty distinguishing between different colors such as red and green. They often prefer black and white or high contrast colors. Your baby will develop *color preference* and you can know these preferences by checking his stares – bright colors (e.g. red/blue) or muted shades. Most babies prefer the stronger colors.
- Mastering of other visual skills includes: **adjusting sight to different distances, following moving objects** and the ability to **perceive depth**.

2.4 Language & Hearing

Many researchers believe that by the fourth month of age, babies understand all the basic sounds that make up the native language. From now until approximately their 6th month, he will develop the ability to master some vocal sounds such as *"mama"* or *"dada"*, yet he is unable to connect the sound with the parent. The following outlines some of the developmental characteristics of hearing and language:

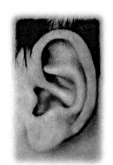

- Participates in back and forth imitations (e.g. if you say "boo," he will try to say it too); promote your child's Sense of communication through sound imitations so that he may learn the importance and effects of using language
- Responds to you by making sounds and moving arms and legs
- Most sounds are consonants that will build into words in the next few months
- Your baby's shape of his mouth will change for sounds
- Able to hear well (almost like an adult)
- Identifies the source of noises and responds to music
- Turns head towards the source of sounds

2.5 Socio-Emotional Development

Your baby is now able to realize that you are a human being, separate from him.

- **Plays with his hands and feet** for a few minutes at a time and this may amuse him with this play.
- **Use social gestures** such as moving his arms to signal to the caregiver to pick him up.
- **Understands** which behavior is acceptable and which is not.
- The smile is developing and he is able to **show real pleasure** when he sees family members or familiar faces.
- **Laughs aloud** (e.g. when tickled or when playing a game) **and cries** when fun activities are ended (e.g. when game is over).

- **Interested in their reflections** in the mirror and some may even smile to their reflection.
- By the end of the fourth month, he can **squeal with pleasure** and is excited by the sight of food.
- He may be **picky about the company around him** when he used to smile at everyone that came in contact at an earlier age. However, he may simply need time to get comfortable with unfamiliar people and objects.
- Interacts with noisy and boisterous older children when he is in the safety of your arms
- **Moods may change** rapidly, laughing one minute and crying the next – this is normal.

2.6 Cognitive Development

At the age of four months, infants are able to retain memory for up to 5-7 minutes. This is clearly shown by their **imitative** skills i.e. able to copy what you do. They are able to participate in back and forth imitation games (e.g. you say book, and he will try to say it back). They may start to discover **cause and effect** (e.g. if you give a light rattle and watch his delight in the sounds it makes when he shakes it), and **object permanence**. Color differences become clearer and may show preference to bright primary colors.

2.7 Additional Developmental Aspects

SLEEPING

- Establish a bedtime routine.
- Most babies will sleep through the night (most do by three months of age).
- Always put the baby to sleep on his back.
- Place infants to sleep when they are drowsy but awake.
- Avoid rocking your baby to sleep or holding him until he falls asleep since he needs to learn to fall asleep on his own.
- Try to ignore him when is squirming or whimpering since he will probably be able to go back to sleep on his own.
- Alternate the position of his head so that he does not sleep on one side.

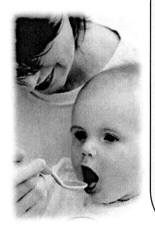

FEEDING

- While solids are started in some countries at 4 months, the CPS (Canadian Pediatric Society) & the AAP (American Academy of Pediatrics) recommends starting solids at 6 months for breastfeeding mothers.
- Milk remains the most important food source.
- Never put him to bed with a bottle in his mouth.
- Feeding should occur 4-6 times /day.
- A private / quiet area is necessary for feeding as he is easily distracted by sights and sounds.
- Consult your doctor about vitamins and fluoride.

Please refer to "Baby and Toddler – Feeding and Nutritional Health"
By: Dr. Maurice Levy

SAFETY

- Do not leave your baby unattended such as in a bath or on high places (tables, beds, sofas or chairs) since he is more active at this stage
- Always keep one hand on your baby.
- Continue using infant car seats properly and securely.
- Ensure a smoke-free environment.
- Never shake his head vigorously.
- Do not place any strings or necklaces around your baby's neck and do not use a string to attach the pacifier to the baby.
- Never hold your baby while drinking a hot liquid.
- At this age, everything goes to the baby's mouth so keep small parts/toys out of reach

ORAL HEALTH

- There is usually an increased amount of saliva at this age, making your baby's face and neck wet; as a result, rashes sometimes develop in the face.
- Use Vaseline or other ointments after discussing this with your doctor.
- Saliva increase is usually due to teeth eruption with first teeth appearing around six months of age.
- Drooling is quite common and does not necessarily indicate early teething; it is probably due to a lot of saliva that the baby has not yet learned to swallow.

3. ENHANCING DEVELOPMENT

Remember to continue holding, cradling, talking, singing and rocking your baby as much as you can. Now is the time to offer him a playpen and some suitable toys to keep him entertained. The following are ways you can enhance your child's development.

a) **Talk** to your child as much as possible to stimulate language and communicative skills (e.g. sing in various pitches, repeat rhymes, converse when feeding or dressing, etc).
b) Babies enjoy feeling different textures of various objects. As such, allow him to **enjoy touching and feeling** various textures (e.g. feathers, satins, cloth, wool). In addition make him reach or grasp for these objects.

c) **Imitate** speech sounds, facial expressions and various movements your child commits (e.g. coos, signs, smiles). This will encourage your child to imitate you as well.
d) **Place brightly colored toys** in front of him when he is lying on his stomach to encourage him to raise his head and push up with his forearms. Throughout the day, be sure to change his position so he learns to alternate between them.
e) Allow him to have some **quiet time on his own** for a little while each day. This will allow him to focus on his surroundings and explore the world around. You can make him feel safe and secure by maintaining eye contact, massaging, holding close, talking, singing, etc.
f) Babies sometimes tend to **show more interest in toys** than people. Some babies even develop an attachment to a particular toy, however this is done more so at later stages of life.
g) Allow your child to experiment by **offering numerous toys** with various qualities (e.g. books that have pop-ups, toys that play music, toys that move on wheels, etc).

4. DEVELOPMENTAL SCREENING AND RED FLAGS

It is important to review and repeat developmental screenings at every age of your child's life in order to assess progression, regression, or any difficulties. Developmental skills are expected to be mastered by the appropriate age in about 85% of children. Although each child is unique, some children have not yet mastered a skill due to various contributing factors such as developmental problems, lack of opportunity to learn or practice, cultural norms, parent/child interaction, environmental limitations or prematurity (i.e. premature infants may develop later than their peers).

Review the following developmental screening to assess your child's development. If you check one or more "no" responses or a *red flag* is present, then discuss with your child's health professional.

PHYSICAL DEVELOPMENT

Gross Motor Skills:
- Lifts head by 90 degrees when lying on the stomach and support self on forearms
- Head is steady when supported in a sitting position
- Turns head from side to side to follow an object past midline

Fine Motor Skills:
- Brings both hands to his chest and keeps his head midline when lying on his back
- Brings hands together when in a supine position
- Holds object when placed in his hands for a brief period of time
- Pulls objects close to his mouth

YES	NO

LANGUAGE, SPEECH AND HEARING

Receptive Skills:
- Turns towards the source of noise
- Smiles upon hearing your voice
- Jumps upon hearing loud voices
- Stops activities and attends closely to unfamiliar sounds

Expressive Skills:
- Coos when content
- Takes turns cooing in response to other cooing
- Randomly babbles
- Use different cries for different needs
- Makes sounds when looking at peoples and toys

YES	NO

COGNITIVE DEVELOPMENT

- Participates in back and forth imitation games (e.g. You say "book" and he will try to say it back)
- Seems to discover cause and effect (e.g. shake the keys and he notices the sound)

YES	NO

SOCIO-EMOTIONAL DEVELOPMENT

- Squeals with joy
- Responds to familiar voice by making sounds and moving arms/legs
- Laughs aloud and smiles at you when you come into view
- Uses social gestures (e.g. lifts arms to be picked up)
- Shows real pleasure when seeing familiar faces (interest in people and surroundings)
- Able to be comforted

YES	NO

For the following "Definite Red Flags", consult you child health professional, if one or more or your answers is "yes".

DEFINITE RED FLAGS

- Stiff or floppy
- Persistent fist clenching
- Poor head control
- Eyes are crossed most of the time

YES	NO

Please note that developmental screening checklists are not 100% or case sensitive. As such, always consult with your child's health professional regarding any developmental concerns.

PARENT CONCERN

My baby is four months old. He sees and hears okay, but he does not bring his hand to the middle and I don't like to move his hands. What should I do?

First, you should consult your doctor to ensure that there are no neurological problems. Once this is done, you may try to stimulate your baby by trying the following:

- Offer toys with different colors
- Offer different toys than the ones he usually plays with
- Provide objects that have different textures and move his hands forwards, middle and around so that he can see
- Play "patty-cake" and have fun with clapping

Development: 5 Months

1. GENERAL

2. DEVELOPMENTAL MILESTONES

2.1 PHYSICAL DEVELOPMENT

2.2 SPEECH, LANGUAGE & COMMUNICATION

2.3 COGNITIVE DEVELOPMENT

2.4 SOCIO-EMOTIONAL DEVELOPMENT

3. ENHANCING DEVELOPMENT

4. DEVELOPMENTAL SCREENING & RED FLAGS

1. GENERAL

During the fifth month, we see the beginning of progressive movement in the baby's motor ability / activity, the widening of visual interests (e.g. spotting small objects and tracking movements), listening skills, speech (better communication), and the development of new curiosities. At this stage, the baby has a relatively larger attention span and is able to stay alert and responsive for a greater period of time. There is increased dynamic interaction and a stronger attachment to the parent/caregiver.

2. DEVELOPMENTAL MILESTONES

2.1 Physical Development

Head / Neck	<ul><li>Able to stabilize his head and hold it well while sitting and in the upright position</li><li>Head kept in line with the rest of his body when pulled to a sitting position</li><li>Head and neck turns to source of any sounds/noises</li></ul>
Body	<ul><li>Able to open arms and legs, lift head and chest</li><li>While arching his back when lying on his stomach, chest is raised and supported by the arms</li><li>Rolls from stomach onto back (a one-way motion)</li><li>Lifts head and shoulders when placed on back</li><li>May even sit momentarily without assistance (sit nearby to provide support; support the baby with pillows to cushion a possible fall)</li></ul>
Arms / Legs	<ul><li>Crawls into crib or on the floor while on his tummy (kicks legs and makes a "swimming" motion with his arms); able to do this maneuver in reverse or move in an intentional manner</li><li>Brings legs to mouth and grabs or sucks his toes</li><li>May be able to pull himself up after sitting to a standing position</li><li>Bounces up and down when you balance his feet on your thighs while supporting him under the arms</li></ul>

Hands	<ul><li>The baby's eyes direct his hands and he tries to reach and touch every object possible, with a good aim too!</li><li>Places toys in mouth wanting to taste or start chewing it</li><li>Holds a bottle with one or both hands; can also grasp and play with a rattle in his hands</li><li>*Comment*: Your baby can transfer an object from one hand to the other or hold it in both hands. Grasping is much stronger and he is now able to resist adults who want to take a toy away from him.</li></ul>

TIP: ORAL EXPLORATIONS
- Nerves and muscles in the baby's mouth including lips and tongue are highly sensitive (even at birth) and can transmit a lot of information. Since the desire to put objects in the mouth is the result of a need to explore, babies will put everything in the mouth to learn about objects.
- By the end of the 5th month, babies start to put objects into their mouth. When this starts, you may be reassured that it is due to the teething process (which coincides simultaneously).
- It is important to watch your baby since there is the risk of putting objects in the mouth that are a choking hazard or dirty (transmitting germs).
- By the age of one year, your child will lose interest in placing objects in the mouth. Babies will shift their attention to learn through with their eyes and hands, using the mouth to eat and gradually, to communicate.

2.2 SPEECH, LANGUAGE AND COMMUNICATION

Your baby now listens with great attention to the world around him. He expresses a range of sounds based on various needs. He also responds to numerous sounds, voices and noises, while trying to seek the source. The human voice always attracts his attention. Babbling is common at this stage including a combination of vowel and consonants such as *GAGA, BABA, MAMA, DADA*, etc. The letters **P – B – M** are the first to appear.
Moreover, the baby may watch your mouth when you speak to try and imitate or utter consonant sounds such as the M and B letters. As such, vocal play can be an entertaining activity in itself. For example, if your baby wants attention, he will babble away to get it!

MORE TO KNOW: Pre-Verbal Communication Development
The course of pre-verbal communicative development is marked by three major transitions within the first year of life:

- The first transition occurs around **two months** of age when infants begin to communicatively interact with others. This is a sudden change that is as evident as birth itself!
- The second transition occurs later in the **fifth month** of life when infants suddenly appear to lose interest in face-to-face interaction with adults. Rather, objects that can be manipulated engross infants.
- The third transition is less obvious and occurs around **9-10 months** of age. Your baby begins to express "real" communicative abilities, expressing interest in various objects, and surroundings.

> **BABY FAVORITE**: Many babies enjoy placing their feet in their mouth and prefer sucking on their toes, rather than sucking on their fingers.

2.3 Cognitive Development

Your baby is now **aware** of certain people including siblings and parents, and is now **beginning to interact with his surroundings**. He may even start playing little games, **understanding the cause, effects and results of simple actions**. For example, he may try throwing something and bending to look for it or watching you to see how you pick it up. Basically, your baby is learning to anticipate actions and is able to mimic sounds, gestures and cadence of your home language. Also, your baby is starting to **sort out the differences** in colours.

2.4 Socio-Emotional Development

Your baby interacts with the world now and expects the world to interact with him.

- He can now let you know when he is **angry, bored or happy.**
- If your baby is anxious, he is able to pull, pinch or scratch his body parts.
- A **strong attachment** to you as the caregiver begins (e.g. the baby raises his arms if he wants to be picked up or cries if you leave the room). He may **act shy** with a stranger or cry if someone other than those familiar to him picks him up.
- May **play alone** and may talk to himself for a long period of time.

- Many babies enjoy a singing box that they can make-work on their own or may enjoy playing with keys.
- Babies love bath toys.
- If your baby is able to sit in a stroller, a trip may be pleasurable.
- Sensitive to the way you act with him.
- Babbling and squealing is endless.

3. ENHANCING DEVELOPMENT

PHYSICAL	<ul><li>Allow him to lie on his stomach, so that he can lift his head up. This is a good exercise to strengthen the neck and back muscles.</li><li>Place a toy in front of him to encourage him to raise his head when he is lying on his stomach. If he is in a sitting position, he will strain to lean toward the object, especially if it is in front of him.</li><li>The floor is an important place for the baby, as he is becoming more mobile (WATCH: Nothing extra should be on the floor for him to easily place in his mouth).</li><li>Allow him to explore your face and body (e.g. tugging ears, patting chin).</li></ul>
SOCIO-EMOTIONAL	<ul><li>Sing to your baby and repeat rhymes.</li><li>Let him listen to different sounds (e.g. birds, wind, etc).</li><li>Playing a game such as "*peek-a-boo*" will allow your baby to understand that when an object is not seen, it is not necessarily gone forever.</li><li>Provide your baby with objects that will stimulate him.</li><li>Stimulate your baby to play freely, because this will awaken his curiosity and sense of ownership.</li><li>Give your baby time to adjust to new persons and to explore new situations.</li></ul>
COGNITIVE	<ul><li>Allow him to observe plenty of colorful pictures. Show pictures of various objects familiar to his environment.</li><li>Do not be quick to resolve frustrating situations for your baby. Interfere only when the baby's goal is impossible (e.g. unable to reach his pacifier).</li></ul>

SPEECH & LANGUAGE 	• Talk to him daily in short, simple sentences and give him enough time to respond. Repeat names daily of any toys, body parts, etc. Accompany these words with actions (e.g. "gone" when finished eating; invent games involving different parts of the body). This will exercise his communication skills. • He will babble, so make sure you are aware of his demands. Try to understand what he is telling you and respond in a simple and coherent way. This will give him confidence. • Continue talking, reading and singing to him. This is a very crucial time and he will begin forming his own words soon. The more you repeat words and the more you say, the quicker he will be able to understand and speak them.

TIP: The Right Baby Toys

- By this stage, your baby can distinguish bold colors and can roll over. He is not only aware of his hands and feet, but amuses himself by playing with them.
- Not too long ago, your baby was able to turn his head only towards the caretaker's voice; now, he will turn his head toward other familiar voices and noises, especially since he is now able to recognize his own name.

- Babies like noises and lights. Great toys can be anything that makes sounds such as little toy phones, rattles, talking or singing dolls, etc.
- Also, he may be able to sit without support. Placing a mobile with dangling objects when your baby is in a sitting position will encourage him to sit up from a lying position to play with the hanging toys. (See chapter on Toys).

4. DEVELOPMENTAL SCREENING AND RED FLAGS

It is important to review and repeat developmental screenings at every age of your child's life in order to assess progression, regression, or any difficulties. Developmental skills are expected to be mastered by the appropriate age in 85% of children. Although each child is unique, some children have not yet mastered a skill due to various contributing factors such as developmental problems, lack of opportunity to learn or practice, cultural norms, parent/child interaction, environmental limitations or prematurity (i.e. premature infants may develop later than their peers).

Review the following developmental screening to assess your child's development. If you check one or more "no" responses or a *red flag* is present, then discuss with your child's health professional.

PHYSICAL DEVELOPMENT

Gross Motor Skills:
- Able to open his arms and legs, lift head and chest when lying on stomach
- Stabilizes head and holds it well while sitting and when in the upright position
- Rolls over from stomach onto back
- Able to bounce up and down when supported under arms and balance feet on your thighs

Fine Motor Skills:
- Tries to reach for object with a good aim
- Directs eyes and hands to touch and reach for objects
- Grasps and plays with rattle in hands
- Able to hold a bottle with one or both hands
- Pulls objects close to his mouth

YES	NO

COGNITIVE DEVELOPMENT

- Begins to interact with surroundings and others (e.g. parents/siblings)
- Understands cause and effect relationships (e.g. throws a toy and begins looking for it)

YES	NO

SPEECH, LANGUAGE AND COMMUNICATION

Receptive Skills:
- Responds to own name
- Watches your face when you talk
- Fascinated by toys that make sounds
- Enjoys nursery rhymes

Expressive Skills:
- Babbles rhythmically (e.g. "dada, gaga, mama")
- Makes noise or gestures to get attention
- Makes return sounds when you talk
- Expresses a range of sounds based on various needs
- Smiles at you and other family members
- Squeals in delight

YES	NO

SOCIO-EMOTIONAL DEVELOPMENT

- Plays alone or talks to himself
- Attached to caregiver (e.g. cries if you leave the room)
- Enjoys a singing box that he can make work on his own

YES	NO

For the following "Definite Red Flags", consult your child health professional, if one or more of your answers is "yes"

DEFINITE RED FLAGS

- Does not respond to sounds in his surroundings
- Does not turn his head to locate sounds
- Shows no affection for caregivers
- Reaches out with only one hand
- Floppy head, especially when pulling up to a sitting position
- Stiffness and tight muscles
- Eyes turn in and out for one or both eyes

YES	NO

Please note that developmental screening checklists are not 100% or case sensitive. As such, always consult with your child's health professional regarding any developmental concerns.

Development: 6 Months

1. GENERAL

2. DEVELOPMENTAL MILESTONES

2.1 PHYSICAL DEVELOPMENT

2.2 SOCIO-EMOTIONAL DEVELOPMENT

2.3 COGNITIVE DEVELOPMENT

2.4 SPEECH AND LANGUAGE DEVELOPMENT

2.5 HEARING AND VISION

2.6 SELF-HELP ADAPTIVE SKILLS

2.7 ADDITIONAL DEVELOPMENTAL ASPECTS

3. ENHANCING DEVELOPMENT, PARENTING & BEHAVIOUR

4. DEVELOPMENTAL SCREENING & RED FLAGS

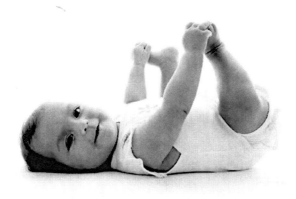

1. GENERAL

The six-month old child experiences various exciting changes and is full of boundless energy, becoming a virtual wiggle worm. Each baby is unique and may be different in concentrating on various things. One may concentrate on trying to talk; another will spend time analyzing toys and objects. Your six-month-old enjoys more "action" and more mobility than ever before.

Your baby will be able to sit on her own and gain a whole new perspective on the world around her. She understands the world of cause and effect (e.g. the six month old discovers that letting go of something is as much fun as picking it up). Eye contact becomes a prominent characteristic at this phase (replacing physical contact). There is a sudden awareness in her surroundings, loving to play in face-to-face interaction with others and developing a sense of trust. Most parents excitedly report that they can hold "conversations" with their infants, taking turns vocalizing and listening.

2. DEVELOPMENTAL MILESTONES
2.1 PHYSICAL DEVELOPMENT

Supine and lifts legs

HEAD & NECK
- Supine position: Raises the head to look at her feet
- Turns head from side to side to look around while sitting
- Prone Position: Lifts head and chest well up, supported on flattened palms and extended arms
- Moves head and eyes in any direction when attention is attracted

BODY/TRUNK

- By the end of 6 months, many are able to sit by themselves. Some may sit alone momentarily, for most though, mild support may still be needed.
- Your baby may particularly like to roll and turn to each side (can roll from their front to back and vice versa)
- Baby begins to 'tripod'-sit with one hand on the ground for support
- Can move in reverse, before being able to advance
- Able to crawl (not ready on all four though)

Prone, arms extended

LEGS

- Lifts legs into vertical position
- Kicks strongly with legs
- Held standing on her feet while bearing weight on feet and bounces
- Can stand holding onto someone or something
- Can pull up to a standing position from a sitting position
- Begins preparation to walk (may want your help to stand; if you hold her under the arm, she may try to bounce)

HANDS

- Hand coordination is improving
- Hand control is developed enough so that she can move an object towards her, however finger coordination is not yet precise
- Tries to take small size things, but not successfully (does better with large objects and can place one cube on top of the other; you may show her how to do this first)
- Likes to shake every toy she takes in her hands and finds out what types of noises it can make (though she believes it is her own hand that is producing the noise and not the object itself)
- Enjoys dropping toys to floor to hear sound of their falls and to see if each time it falls, the same thing happens
- Able to hold a cup with hands
- Uses whole hands and passes toys from one hand to the other
- Takes everything into mouth
- Grasps and reaches for small toys
- Picks up object with any part of thumb or fingers

Held standing & takes weight on legs

2.2 Socio-Emotional Development

The six-month-old baby:

- Learns to **express various emotions**
- Understands by your tone and **uses/responds to various facial expressions**
- Still **friendly with strangers** but occasionally shows some shyness or even anxiety when approaches too nearly or abruptly
- Has sudden mood changes and various emotions (pleasure, anger, etc)
- May cry if left in the middle of a game
- Likes to "examine" your face (e.g. run her finger by your eye, nose, mouth, etc)
- Enjoys **playing with adults** that are familiar to her
- If offered a rattle, she will reach for it and shake it deliberately to make sounds
- Manipulate objects attentively and passes it from hand to hand
- **Objects** if you take toys away
- **Laughs and squeals** aloud in play
- Discovers herself & smiles in the mirror; and loves having conversations with her new "little friend"
- Vocalizes pleasure and displeasure (e.g. some babies touch their genitals, and it gives them pleasure – this is natural, so let them do so)

TIP: Child Behaviour and Your Attention/ Reaction
Your baby is also learning that her behaviors (both the ones you like and the ones you don't) engage you, so starting now and for years to come, your child will do just about anything to get your attention. As she gets older, she may get into mischief to provoke a reaction from you.

Did You Know: Picking Babies Up
When your baby wants to be picked up, she will not only use her voice but she will gesture with raised arms and form a proud sitting position.

2.3 Cognitive Development

The six-month old baby:

- Behavior is more planned
- Enjoys looking at toys upside down to have different perspectives
- Able to compare between two toys
- Will want you to repeat her favorite game
- Attention span is increased considerably now
- Able to recall objects and people most of the time
- Begins to build a grasping knowledge of cause and effect relationships
- Continues to rely on her mouth to learn about objects and begins hand exploration
- Clearly understands a few words
- Able to recognize each parent
- Listens carefully as you recite her favorite rhyme or song
- Likes to compare sounds of various toys

2.4 Speech and Language Development

The communication skills of your baby are rapidly expanding. It is evidenced by her **squeals, bubbling sounds, operative octave changes**, and so forth. She is now interested in **producing new sounds**, where she now has more control over what comes out of her mouth. She may have developed a vocabulary of sounds that she makes when greeting familiar faces in the morning or when you are leaving her. She can use some **vowel sounds or single/ double syllables** such as "a-a, goo, muh", etc. There are certainly long babbly sentences that she makes, trying to have a conversation with you and others. Also, she can now **recognize different tones and inflections** and may even cry if you speak to her harshly.

2.5 Hearing and Vision

HEARING
- Enjoys sounds (especially ones that toys make)
- Probably turns head immediately upon the sound of noise to find its source
- Attentive to sounds she hears
- Particularly enjoys music
- Turns immediately to the mothers or caregivers voice across the room
- Shows evidence of selective responses to different emotional tones of voice
- Responds to own name

VISION
- Eagerly moves eyes when attention is attracted
- Follows adults activity across the room with purposeful alertness
- Eyes are more in union with one another (squints are abnormal)
- Fixates on interesting small objects within 6-12 inches (may almost simultaneously stretch out both hands to grasp these objects)
- Watches a round ball of 2 ¼ inches at ten feet
- If a toy falls, she will follow it to its resting place unless it falls outside of vision range (then she will forget about it)

TIP: Eye Colour

- By now, you may be able to see your child's possible permanent eye color. Inherited genes from the parents and even the grandparents determine eye color.
- The genes for eye color determine the amount of melanin, a dark brown pigment, which is produced. Melanin production generally increases during the 1st year of life, leading to a deepening of eye color. The color is often stable by about 6 months of age. However, the genetics of eye colors inheritance is not a cut and dry matter as was once thought. Blue-eyed parents have been known (rarely though) to have a brown-eyed child and people can even have eyes of two colours!
- Typically, final eye color can be reached by 6-12 months of age; however 10-15% of eye colors continue to change well into adulthood.

2.6 SELF-HELP ADAPTIVE SKILLS

Your baby can now feed herself such foods as crackers and may even be able to enjoy eating with her hands.

2.7 ADDITIONAL DEVELOPMENTAL ASPECTS

FEEDING

- At this age, babies like to eat with their hands and enjoy the touch of food. They like to squeeze, mix it, etc. It is certainly not the time to teach your child cleanliness habits.
- As the amount of solid food intake increases, the amount of breast milk or formula use decreases.
- Most babies are developmentally ready for solid foods but when and how much you give your child depends on whether your baby is ready.
- Rice cereal is the first solid started and less likely to cause allergy.
- When starting a new food space the time apart between a few days and introduce one at a time to check for allergy.
- Allow her to feed herself some of the time. She will now develop clear preferences for various foods.
- Allow your child to use a spoon. Start using a cup since it is important to eliminate bottles by the baby's first birthday. She will not be able to hold it up by herself.

SAFETY

- Now that she is more active, you need to ensure that play places are safer.
- Provide a safe environment that is relaxing and allows her to explore environment
- Never leave her alone or on high surface unsupervised
- Continue to use the infant car seat and ensure that it is properly secured at all times.
- Maintain a carbon monoxide detector and smoke detector.
- Keep a smoke-free environment in your home.
- Empty baths or small pools immediately after use.
- Avoid over-exposure to the sun.
- Do not leave heavy objects or containers of hot liquids on tables with a tablecloth that your baby may pull down.
- Plug in electrical sockets.
- Keep toys with small parts or sharp toys out of reach.
- Lower the crib mattress.

SLEEP

- Most babies take at least 2 naps during the day at this age
- Ensure she has a good bedtime routine and has developed proper sleep association.
- Encourage her to console herself by putting her to sleep awake.
- Some six-month old babies decrease the length and/or frequency of naps.
- Due to the emergence of separation anxiety, the six-month old babies may show resistance to naps and sleeping at night. Some begin night awakening for short periods of time. If this happens, check your baby but keep the visits brief.

TIP: Bowel Movements & Fussing
Your baby has her own frequency of bowel movements. Some will strain, grunt and fuss when they have bowel movements. This does not mean that they are constipated.

MORE TO KNOW: Teething
If your child's teething is delayed do not be worried as children have their own timetable. The process of teething is different for each baby. Be prepared to notice your child "gnaw" on everything when her teeth are ready to come out!

3. ENHANCING DEVELOPMENT, PARENTING AND BEHAVIOUR

a) Place the baby on her stomach and place a toy in front of her to encourage her to push up on her hands, as she will try to **reach for the toy**.
b) **Place toys in various positions** and distance them from the baby. This will allow her to understand that she must **reach out and grab the toy** if she wants it. You can help by saying the name of the toy and telling her to go on and get it.
c) Encourage your baby to roll from her stomach onto her back. Help her understand how her body works and allow her to **explore the environment**.
d) Encourage your baby to **play and kick** with her feet and legs.
e) To improve your child's sitting position, prop your baby up in the v-shape on your extended legs to help her get accustomed to this new position. If your baby is still on the chubby side a little bit, it may be more difficult for her to keep her balance right now.

f) **Vary your child's position** by placing her on the stomach, on the back, in a supported sitting position and so forth.
g) Stimulate your child's senses by allowing her to explore and place safe things around her **to touch and manipulate**.
h) Make your baby **imitate** sounds as though you are having a conversation.
i) Call or **make noises** from different parts of the room to help your baby understand that she must look at the direction of new sounds.
j) **Show various actions** such as waving goodbye or blowing a kiss for the baby to learn it by herself.
k) **Try to understand** what your baby means by looking, reaching, babbling, crying, etc.
l) **Comfort your baby** when she is unhappy or fussy by rocking, holding or talking to her in a soft voice. Respond when she cries since there is no such thing as spoiling the young child.

m) **Daily interaction** provide opportunities for her to focus and recognize concepts from others
n) **Expose** your baby to a variety of different people during social outings and teach him to say hello and goodbye.
o) **Teach cause and effect** relationships of objects (e.g. ask "who could be at the door?" when the doorbell rings, etc).
p) To improve language and development skills, **talk to your baby** about what happened throughout the day, respond to sounds and mimic your baby's coos.
q) To further develop language skills, **speak slowly and clearly** to your child. Give your child time to respond to you. Use short sentences and identify objects. Focus on repetition by singing the same songs and reciting the same nursery rhyme.
r) Remain particularly **sensitive** to her moods. Babies need to know that you are there for them. If you leave the room and she begins crying, call her from another room with reassuring words that you are nearby and that you will return shortly.
s) Continue to **read books** to your baby and ask simple questions about the books you read.
t) **Play various games** with your child such as peek-a-boo, patty-cake and body games.
u) **Begin setting limits** for future discipline by using distraction, reducing stimulation and establishing routines. Ensure that your baby is learning self-soothing techniques by providing your child with the same transitional objects such as a stuffed animals or favorite blanket or toy.

4. DEVELOPMENTAL SCREENING AND RED FLAGS

It is important to review and repeat developmental screenings at every age of your child's life in order to assess progression, regression, or any difficulties. Developmental skills are to be mastered by the appropriate age in 85% of children. Although each child is unique, some children have not yet mastered a skill due to various contributing factors such as developmental problems, lack of opportunity to learn or practice, cultural norms, parent/child interaction, environmental limitations or prematurity (i.e. premature infants may develop later than their peers). Review the following developmental screening to assess your child's development. If you check one or more "no" responses or a *red flag* is present, then discuss with your child's health professional.

PHYSICAL DEVELOPMENT

Gross Motor Skills:
- Makes attempts to roll over from back to stomach or stomach to back
- Keeps head level/vertically positioned when pulled to a sitting position
- Sits well without support

Fine Motor Skills:
- Transfers object from one hand to another
- Uses each hand to reach for toys or familiar persons
- Brings hands or toys to mouth

YES	NO

SOCIO-EMOTIONAL DEVELOPMENT

- Interacts with others and shows interest in interactions
- Smiles and laughs in response to your smiles and laughter – shows full range of emotions
- Imitates sounds you make or babbles to converse with you – imitated interaction by smiling or vocalizing
- Alert to surroundings

YES	NO

COGNITIVE DEVELOPMENT

- Seems to understand some words (e.g. Bye-bye, Daddy)
- Begins to understand cause and effect relativity (e.g. shaking a rattle to make a sound; discovering that letting something go is as much fun as picking it up)
- Able to recall objects and people most of the time
- Discriminates strangers from familiar people

YES	NO

SPEECH, LANGUAGE AND COMMUNICATION

Receptive Skills:

- Responds to own name
- Watches your face when you talk
- Fascinated by toys that make sounds
- Enjoys nursery rhymes
- Recognizes a few tones and inflections

YES	NO

Expressive Skills:

- Babbles rhythmically, uses vowel, singe/double syllables
- Makes noise or gestures to get attention
- Makes return sounds when you talk to her (try to make conversation by babbling or talking gibberish)
- Smiles at you and other family members

YES	NO

VISION AND HEARING

- Follows moving objects with eyes
- Startles in responds to loud noise
- Turns to face the source of strange noise
- Looks to the floor when dropping toys

YES	NO

For the following "Definite Red Flags", consult your child health professional, if one or more of your answers is "yes".

DEFINITE RED FLAGS

	YES	NO
Loss of any previously obtained skills in any developmental domain		
Rarely engage socially (e.g. smiling, eye contact)		
More interested in looking at objects than people		
No babbling		
Difficulties swallowing or feeding		
Legs are stiffly extended or places no weight on legs, only toes		

Please note that developmental screening checklists are not 100% or case sensitive. As such, always consult with your child's health professional regarding any developmental concerns.

TIP: Cooing and Babbling
In early infancy, cooing and gurgling, is totally random. Eventually you will notice that certain coos and gurgles are directed right at you when you are talking with your baby. Between the first few weeks of life and the second month, babies make the vowel sounds (i.e. a, e, i, o, u). By about 4 months of age, babies will add a loud laugh and squeal along with a few consonants. When babies begin experimenting with consonants, they tend to repeat some simple combinations such as, "ba" or "da". Following the two syllables, 1 consonant sound, (e.g. a-ga, a-ba) are strings of consonants called "babbling" (e.g. dadadadadada).
By eight months of age, many babies can produce word like double consonants such as, "da-da, ma-ma, ba-ba".

Development: 7 Months

1. General

2. Developmental Milestones

2.1 Physical Development

2.2 Speech and Language Development

2.3 Cognitive Development

2.4 Social Development

2.5 Vision

3. General Developmental Aspects

4. Red Flags

1. GENERAL

- At the age of 7 months, babies are able to show more attention, concentration and interest in details.
- Infants begin to show a sense of independence by crawling, rolling from one side to the other, developing fine motor skills, teeth showing and so forth.

2. DEVELOPMENTAL MILESTONES

2.1 Physical Development

HEAD / NECK	• Holds his head up
TRUNK / BACK	• Sits without hand support • May be able to sit on a high chair • May be able to get into a sitting position from lying down on the stomach by pushing up on his arms • Pulls up to stand from a sitting position • Creeps or crawls
LEGS	• Bears weight on his legs when held upright • Stands on both legs while holding onto someone • Walks holding onto furniture (cruising) • Moves backwards and forwards when standing on legs • Loves bouncing
FINE MOTOR SKILLS	• Explores with hands and mouth • Starts to use his finger instead of the palm • Transfers objects from one hand to the other • Picks up objects with any part of the thumb and finger (using grasp, not the pincer grasp) • Lifts, shakes, pushes, rolls or throws objects • Waves bye-bye or claps with hands • Imitates others actions • Holds 2 toys with his hands separately • May grab a toy using only 1 hand • Sips from a 2-handle cup with your assistance • May try to feed himself with his fingers or a small spoon

2.2 SPEECH AND LANGUAGE DEVELOPMENT
Your 7 month old baby presents the following speech and language developments:
- States "mama" and "dada" indiscriminately
- Responds to own name
- Distinguishes emotions by the tone of the voice
- Responds to sounds by making sounds
- Imitates noises or sounds
- Uses voice to express anger or joy

2.3 COGNITIVE DEVELOPMENT
- Finds hidden objects and actively enjoys hiding games (e.g. Jack in the Box)
- Struggles to get objects that are out of reach
- Understands that he has to reach to bring toys closer
- Begins to understand the meaning of his actions
- Learns the significance of various tones of speech (e.g. bursts into tears when spoken to harshly)
- Learns that objects relate in 3-dimensional spaces

TIP: Authority Defiance
At this age, your baby may begin testing your authority by refusing to follow your directions. He is curious and the best tactic to help him explore his curiosity while being authoritative is to simply say "no" and distract him to another activity.

2.4 SOCIAL DEVELOPMENT
- Wants to be included in social situations
- May fear strangers
- Shows humour
- Wriggles in anticipation of play
- Begins to learn the meaning of the word "no"
- Coos or babbles when happy
- Objects if you try to take a toy away
- Enjoys playing "peek-a-boo"
- Enjoys social play
- Interested in moving images
- Responds to other people expressing emotions
- Likes to play with noisy toys

2.5 VISION
- Looks for dropped objects and able to track moving objects
- Develops full color vision
- Distance vision matures

3. GENERAL DEVELOPMENTAL ASPECTS

Feeding & Nutrition
- ✓ Nutrition becomes more diverse at this age.
- ✓ Continue offering your baby new foods.
- ✓ Introduce one new food at a time when the baby is happy and sociable.
- ✓ Use breast milk and/or formula along with strained solid foods.
- ✓ You can offer cereals and strained vegetables or fruits.

Teething
- ✓ Teething may have already begun as early as 3 months of age or as late as 12 months; though the average is 5-6 months.
- ✓ You can now expect the appearance of 2 upper central incisors then the 2 lateral incisors.
- ✓ Expect increased drooling once your baby starts teething.
- ✓ Sometimes, babies play with the ears because of teeth eruption while others bite or suck their inner lip.

TIP: Enhancing Activities
▪ Your baby will enjoy soft and pleasant toys that are textured, able to hold with a finger and musical toys.
▪ To encourage fine motor activity, place a toy just out of reach and watch your baby try to get it.
▪ Enjoy playing the same game over and over again such as peek-a-boo or patty-cake.

4. RED FLAGS

If you check at least 1 or more of the following red flags, consult your child's health professional.

- Seems stiff with tight muscles
- Seems very floppy
- Head flaps back when he is pulled up to a sitting position
- Reaches with only 1 hand
- Refuses to cuddle
- Shows no affection for the parent or caregiver
- Does not enjoy being around others
- One or both eyes turn in or out consistently
- Does not respond to sounds around him
- Difficulty getting objects to his mouth
- Does not laugh or make squealing sounds by 6 months
- Does not bear some of his own weight
- Shows no interest in games like peek-a-boo or patty-cake

Development: 8 Months

1. General

2. Development

2.1 Physical Development

2.2 Social/Emotional Development

2.3 Cognitive Development

2.4 Speech, Language, and Vision Development

1. GENERAL

The age of 8 months is one full of curiosity, exploration, learning and discovery. Your child's presence is now felt and heard as she is busy pulling, squeezing, chewing, crawling at fast speeds, imitating, and so forth. A significant development at the end of this month is the ability to pick up small objects with the pincer grasp. Thus, it is time to further baby-proof your home.

2. DEVELOPMENT
2.1 PHYSICAL DEVELOPMENT

FINE MOTOR SKILLS (HANDS)	<ul><li>**Points** to new objects (often points with index finger)</li><li>Points and **follows** with her eyes when someone else is pointing at objects</li><li>Learns to **wave bye-bye, clap hands & even "answer" the phone**</li><li>Able to **hold 1 toy and use** it</li><li>Can **bring a small toy towards her and pick** it up</li><li>Easily **uses fingers to pick up** pieces of food and holds it with her fist closed</li><li>**Drinks** from a cup</li><li>Opens hand and uses fingers to drop objects (beginning to master the **pincer grasp** – the delicate movement that allows her to pick up small objects with her thumb and then, fingers)</li></ul>
LEGS	<ul><li>Crawling muscles are getting stronger, so standing is the next attempt</li><li>**Stands alone** for a few seconds</li><li>Once successful at standing, explores abilities with standing situations</li><li>Uses furniture to **lean on and stand**</li><li>**Walks holding** onto furniture</li></ul>
BACK / TRUNK	<ul><li>**Sits well with no support** for longer periods of time</li><li>**Crawls forwards and backwards**</li><li>**Turns** over easily</li><li>Able to get into a **sitting position from her stomach**</li><li>**Pulls up to a standing** position from a seated one</li></ul>

2.2 Social / Emotional Development
The following are social/emotional developments seen in the 8-month-old baby:

- Shows unhappiness when something is taken away
- Plays "peek-a-boo" and "patty-cake"
- May perform tricks (e.g. throwing kisses to familiar people)
- Empathetic (e.g. may start crying when seeing someone else cry)
- Shy or anxious around strangers, especially when tired or cranky
- Socializes with a mirror (a favourite activity), though she does not yet recognize who she is socializing with

TIP: Night time Anxiety
To help your child with night-time anxiety, spend some extra cuddle time with her before bed by reading, snuggling and softly singing together.

2.3 Cognitive Development
The following are cognitive developments of the 8-month-old baby:

- Learns new concepts relating to spatial relationships
- Facial features are more clearly defined
- Understands the meaning of "no"
- Understands how objects relate to one another (e.g. realizes that smaller objects fit into bigger ones)
- Looks at correct pictures when you name them (same thing with objects occur)
- Explores objects by shaking, banging, dropping or throwing them
- Likes to see things fall down

2.4 Speech, Language & Vision Development

Speech & Language
- States "mama" and "dada"
- Communicates using vowels and consonants (e.g. says "ma-ma")

Vision
- Your baby's vision is now almost adult-like in its clarity and depth perception.
- Though her short-range of vision is still great, her long-range vision is good enough to recognize people and objects (even across a room).

3. ENHANCING DEVELOPMENT

1. Offer considerable freedom for exploration.
2. Place scattered pillows to climb over while in the room.
3. Place toys in the corner of a room for her to discover.
4. Roll a ball for her to chase.
5. Let her feed herself to improve head-eye coordination as well as the pincer grasp.
6. Praise her for effort.
7. Offer a magazine for her to rip and have fun with.
8. If she is scared of the vacuum, stop using it and show her how it works.
9. Make play-dates with other children for her.
10. Get on the floor and play with her, showing her what toys can do.
11. Help find comfort in new surroundings.
12. Hug and talk to her softly.
13. Do not push her into situations with others when she is not comfortable. As you approach others, give her little hugs and kisses and quietly let her know who is coming.
14. Accept separation anxiety.
15. Let her take the security object with her if she would like (except for a bottle or juice that can cause tooth decay).

Development: 9 Months

1. GENERAL

2. DEVELOPMENTAL MILESTONES

2.1 PHYSICAL DEVELOPMENT

2.2 COGNITIVE DEVELOPMENT

2.3 SOCIO-EMOTIONAL DEVELOPMENT

2.4 ADDITIONAL DEVELOPMENTAL ASPECTS

3. ENHANCING DEVELOPMENT

4. PARENTING & DISCIPLINE

5. DEVELOPMENTAL SCREENING & RED FLAGS

1. GENERAL

At the age of nine months, babies begin to follow simple instructions. Locomotion abilities improve. New objects, people and environments may scare him and for this reason, he may be especially close to you. Your baby seems to be increasingly busy and happy with his newfound independence (e.g. cruising around furniture, exploring instincts and impulses, practicing and improving achievements). The earliest indication of an emerging identity occurs between 6-9 months of age, when the infant displays interest in his own mirror image.

Your baby begins to understand more complex concepts such as object relation and permanence; more sophisticated play as well as increased finger and hand coordination. Yet, the new and developing maturity that occurs at this age comes with new fears – separation and stranger anxiety. There may be a need for transitional objects that provide comfort to ease separation anxiety. Your child is now beginning to have a mind of his own, so enjoy this time in your baby's life!

2. DEVELOPMENTAL MILESTONES
2.1 PHYSICAL DEVELOPMENT

HEAD/NECK
<ul><li>Able to turn head when crawling</li><li>Follows a rolling ball 1/8th of an inch at 10 feet as well as fallen toys</li><li>Turns to look for a sound</li></ul>
BODY
<ul><li>Able to sit by himself without support</li><li>Pulls up to a standing position from a sitting position, holding onto support for a few minutes but is unable to lower himself</li><li>Able to lean forward to pick up objects</li><li>Crawls up the stairs</li></ul>
ARMS/HANDS
<ul><li>Can build a tower of two cubes</li><li>Able to lift two toys, each in one hand; approaches large toys with two hands; Works to get a toy out of reach</li><li>Picks up objects with any point of thumb and forefinger ("pincer grasp")</li><li>Claps hands and waves bye-bye</li></ul>

- Begins to point at distant objects with fingers
- Can release a toy by dropping it or by pressing against a firm surface, but cannot yet place it down voluntarily

LEGS
- Locomotion ability is improving
- Climbing instincts exist (climbing upstairs is easy while descending the stairs proves dangerous)
- Able to stand with or without support (usually able to stand holding onto furniture) and even sometimes, play with a toy while standing
- Begin cruising (a step before walking)
- Learning how to bend his knees and sit after standing

PINCER GRASP: The emergence of a thumb-finger grasp typically presents around 8-9 months of age and a neat pincer grasp emerges by about 12 months. This skill is used in such tasks as self-feeding and the exploration of small objects

2.2 Cognitive Development

Cognitive developments include the following:

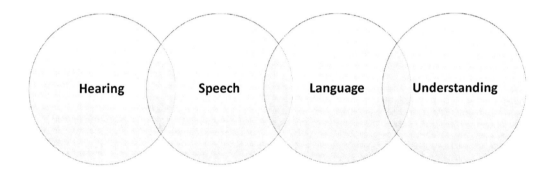

- **Understands** more complex concepts such as **object permanence** (e.g. it is still there, even though it is not in view)
- More **sophisticated** in terms of play
- States "Mama" and "Dada" and able to **say it discriminately** or states one word other than these two
- **Understands** the meaning of "no", but not always obeying it
- May be able to respond to a **one-step command** with a gesture and understands short instructions (e.g. where is the ball?)
- **Vocalizes** deliberately as a means of interpersonal communication

- **Imitates** adults playful vocals and other sounds (e.g. lip-smacking)
- Begins to **understand the relation** between objects (e.g. placing the cover of a pot)
- **Able to pass a toy** through a hole, but is still not ready to adjust to more sophisticated toys
- May be able to **remember** games played the day before
- Able to **protect** himself and his belongings

> **OBJECT PERMANENCE:** A major milestone for the 9-month old baby is the achievement of object permanence (constancy), the understanding that objects continue to exist even when it cannot be seen. At 4-7 months of age, infants look down for a ball that has been dropped, but quickly give up if it is not seen. With object permanence, infants persist in searching for objects hidden under a cloth or behind the caregiver's back.

> **Does My Child Understand Me?**
> Your baby's understanding of words far outpaces her ability to use them and her babbling is probably starting to sound more like real words. Also, at this age, your child understands more from your tone than from your actual words.

2.3 Socio-Emotional Development

- Chooses her own toy to play with and may object if toy is taken away
- **May be sensitive** to other child (e.g. crying if others cry)
- Enjoys the imitation of facial and bodily actions – an "**avid mimic**" (e.g. lip-smacking, coughing)
- May appear in front of the crowd and **repeats actions** (if actions are short-term)
- A "**born performer**" and comedian (e.g. may perform funny actions for others or makes sounds to attract attention)
- **Cries** when separated from the mother
- Clearly **distinguishes strangers** from familiar faces and requires reassurance
- **Name recognition**: Able to respond to her own name by looking around or stopping to see who is calling
- Baby responds to **simple commands**

- Tries to **grasp a spoon** while being fed
- **Throws** the body back and stiffens in annoyance and resistance, while probably vocalizing at the same time
- Prefers to **play close** to the parents, usually in a nearby room, to feel more secure

2.4 ADDITIONAL DEVELOPMENTAL ASPECTS

MORE TO KNOW: Infections at this Age & Maternal Antibodies
Nine months is an age where your child is increasingly prone to infections, probably due to the loss of maternal antibodies during pregnancy. Continue to sanitize all products as well as your hands and those of others who come in contact with your child, and keep all those who are ill away from your child.

PARENTAL CONCERN: Are Shoes Good or Bad?
Shoes are unnecessary, however, some parents enjoy the thrill of additional accessories, such as baby booties. In some cases booties may provide additional warmth in colder conditions.

FEEDING
Nine to twelve months of age is a very important learning period for feeding. By this age, your child should be breastfeeding and/or receiving formula as well as different types of solids (e.g. cereals, vegetables, fruits, meats, dairy, etc).
Solid foods are important to include in the diet to provide your child with the extra nutrients required (e.g. Vitamin D, carbohydrates, etc). Remember to offer a variety of foods and change the texture of the foods to include smooth, pureed foods to more lumpy textures and finger foods.
At this age, many babies begin to chew table foods (teeth are not always necessarily required) and drink from a cup. Continue teaching your baby how to drink from a cup.

SAFETY
- Childproof your home, if this was not already done at the age of 6 months.
- Do not leave him alone in a bath full of water or in any high places such as tables, balconies, sofas, chairs, etc. Always keep one hand on your baby
- Avoid baby walkers as there is a risk of injury and no clear benefits
- Fence any pools and tubs full of water

- Avoid over exposure to the sun or taking your child in the sun between 10 am and 3 pm. Use waterproof sunscreen and an SPF of more than 15
- Plug electrical sockets
- Keep medications and substances that may be of potential risk to a child out of reach
- Learning CPR is suggested in case of choking or an emergency

SLEEP

At 9 months of age, your child may begin waking up at night for short periods of time. When this happens, check your baby to ensure that everything is okay, however, keep the visit short. Avoid stimulating him (e.g. rocking him, reading a book, etc) and learn to leave the room quickly. Do not take him to bed with you or with a bottle. This will only reinforce the night awakening process and it may turn into a habit. Rather, encourage him to console himself by placing him in bed awake. This will teach him that bedtime is a time for sleeping and he has to learn to simply close his eyes and fall asleep.

Resistance to napping and going to sleep may occur due to separation anxiety. Infants who have been sleeping through the night for months may begin to awaken regularly and cry. Your baby may also start to wean himself from the morning nap, which is normal. Discuss any concerns with your child's health professional.

3. ENHANCING DEVELOPMENT

a) You can give your child a push by standing or kneeling in front of him and holding out your hands encouragingly. By holding both hands, you are allowing and helping your child **walk** towards you.
b) Offer your child **toys that stimulate some sort of actions** (e.g. moving parts with wheels, doors that open and close). Also, provide toys that your child can hold and **bang together** (e.g. pots, pans, blocks).
c) Show your child how to throw toys into a container and how to take it out.
d) Place toys on the floor but out of reach and encourage your child to move towards them. While sitting, encourage your baby to reach up and to the side for toys. Help your child practice getting in and out of a sitting position on his own.
e) To help your child **practice using his fingers**, place small finger foods in a bowl and encourage your baby to pick them out.
f) **Become your baby's playmate:** Try to take a toy away from your child and then give it back. You may also try rolling a ball to your baby when you are engaged in "floor" play and see if he rolls it back to you.

g) **Share various activities with your child** including peek-a-boo (cover your face and say "where is mommy?" and then uncover your face and say "peek-a-boo"), face fun (babies love pointing and pulling on facial features so turn this into a game by making funny noises for each feature; repeat the feature to reinforce labels and language – "this is daddy's nose").
h) Offer **a comfort object** such as a blanket, stuffed animal, etc. This helps your baby feel more secure.
i) Constantly **encourage** your child and tell him how wonderful he is and let him feel secure with your words.
j) Allow your child to **hold a book and play** with the pages while you say the names of the pictures.
k) **Teach your child short instructions** to follow by example (e.g. wave bye-bye, blow kisses, clapping hands). Repeat these actions several times.
l) Teach your child **cause and effects** (e.g. turn on the music box and the child will begin to dance).
m) Reinforce recognition of certain behaviors (e.g. responding to name when called).
n) The more you **talk to your child**, the more your baby will learn about **communication**.

*If a particular activity is seen as stressful or frustrating, leave it for another day

4. PARENTING & DISCIPLINE

The following are some helpful hints in parenting your child:
- Your child will begin to get opinionated about almost everything from what foods to eat to when to play, etc. Occasionally, your child's opinion may turn into a protest, so now is the time to **begin setting limits and saying 'no'**.
- Encourage speech development in your child by constantly **chattering with him**.
- **Provide safe opportunities** for your child **to explore** the world and his surroundings.
- **Never "spank" your child**. If you get angry with your child, you may place him in the crib or playpen for 1-2 minutes. This will allow both you and your child to calm down and allows your child to know that he has done something inappropriate or unacceptable.
- Remember that consistency is important.

PARENT CONCERN: Can you discipline a nine-month-old?
You can discipline your child at this age to protect him from danger. Teach your child how to amuse himself and re-orient or distract his attention when trying to discipline him away from behavior that is unacceptable. Unfortunately, you cannot reason with a child at this age and it is possible for children to have a "bad day", the same way we adults do. Simply remember to say "no" firmly, stay calm, and certainly do not impose consequences just because of crying.

5. DEVELOPMENTAL SCREENING AND RED FLAGS

It is important to review and repeat developmental screenings at every age of your child's life in order to assess progression, regression, or any difficulties. Developmental skills are to be mastered by the appropriate age in 85-90% of children. Although each child is unique, some children have not yet mastered a skill due to various contributing factors such as developmental problems, lack of opportunity to learn or practice, cultural norms, parent/child interaction, environmental limitations or prematurity (i.e. premature infants may develop later than their peers). Review the following developmental screening to assess your child's development. If you check one or more "no" responses or a *red flag* is present, then discuss with your child's health professional.

PHYSICAL DEVELOPMENT

Gross Motor Skills:
- Interest in reaching objects
- Stand with support
- Sits Steadily by 9-10 months of age without support
- Rolls over from a supine to prone position
- Cruises around furniture

Fine Motor Skills:
- Transfers toys from one hand to another
- Performs the pincer grasp

YES	NO

YES	NO

SOCIO-EMOTIONAL DEVELOPMENT

- Interest in peek-a-boo or patty-cake type of games
- Searches for hidden objects by 10-12 months of age
- Turns when name is called
- Waves bye-bye or raise his arms to be lifted
- Expresses more than one or two emotions (e.g. happy, sad angry, upset, fear)

YES	NO

HEARING, VISION, AND SPEECH DEVELOPMENTS

Receptive Skills:
- Understands verbal routines
- Listens when spoken to
- Turns and looks at your face when called by names or when speaking
- Recognizes the names of familiar objects
- Responds to requests and visual cues

Expressive Skills:
- Points
- Babbles in imitation of real speech with expression – vocalizes with you
- Vocalization is varied with different types of unusual sounds or sequence length

YES	NO

Please note that developmental screening checklists are not 100% or case sensitive. As such, always consult with your child's health professional regarding any developmental concerns.

For the following "Definite Red Flags", consult your child health care professional, if one or more of your answers is "yes"

DEFINITE RED FLAGS

- Stiff or floppy
- Resistant in making eye contact
- Eyes are always crossed
- Shows little interest in social interaction and smiles infrequently
- Makes unusual vocalization or laughs inappropriately
- Does not point for what he wants or makes intentional 2 person communications
- No babbling, infant squealing or laughing
- Does not state any single words like "mama" or "dada"

YES	NO

Development: 10 Months

1. GENERAL

2. DEVELOPMENTAL MILESTONES

2.1 PHYSICAL DEVELOPMENT

2.2 SOCIO-EMOTIONAL DEVELOPMENT

2.3 COGNITIVE DEVELOPMENT

2.4 SPEECH, LANGUAGE AND ADAPTIVE SELF-HELP

2.5 GENERAL DEVELOPMENT: FEEDING AND SLEEP

3. ENHANCING DEVELOPMENT

1. GENERAL

At the ten-month-old stage, babies search for company and attention. They understand the meaning of the word "no" and even can repeat the word and respond with a head nod. However, your baby may still not stop doing whatever they are not supposed to be doing.

At this age, the baby would willingly like to please the parents, but at the same time, wants to discover the world on his own. Babies are interested in meeting new people, participating in new and exciting activities, and so forth. Although your child enjoys this newfound interest in independence, he still "looks" for permission from the parents for everything. Moreover, only a few ten-month-old children really walk. However, all ten-month-olds are able to sit and change positions, and are attracted to stairs.

2. DEVELOPMENTAL MILESTONES

2.1 Physical Development

GROSS MOTOR SKILLS	<ul><li>Raises himself to a standing position from a sitting position</li><li>May stand without support when letting go of furniture for a moment (able to stand alone and may even be able to do so well)</li><li>May walk with support or holding onto furniture</li><li>Usually able to crawl</li><li>Able to climb up the stairs but usually not down</li><li>May be able to roll a ball back to you or "play ball"</li></ul>
FINE MOTOR SKILLS	<ul><li>Tries to help dress himself</li><li>Picks up objects with fingers</li><li>Able to hold 2 small toys with one hand</li><li>Prefers the use of one hand and one side of the body</li><li>Able to pick-up a Cheerio cereal with the thumb and finger without resting his wrist on a solid surface</li><li>May even be able to pick up a tiny object neatly with the tips of his thumb and forefinger</li><li>Your child may be able to get into a sitting position while lying on the stomach, sit from a standing position, and sits confidently. These are signs of the trunk physically developing.</li></ul>

2.2 Socio-Emotional Development

Your baby is now experiencing a blooming personality that is now beginning to emerge. The socio-emotional development includes:

- **Mimics** the parents / caregiver; imitates the faces and actions of others
- **Vocalizes** to attract attention
- May offer a **broad smile** to anyone he meets or may behave shyly when strangers attempt engaging with him
- **Expresses feelings and needs**; shows mood changes (e.g. sad, happy, angry)
- Expressions comprise more of **gestures and sounds** rather than cries
- **Repeats** sounds and gestures for attention
- Fears strange places and situations
- Objects when a toy is taken away
- **Preference** for certain toys over others
- Able to **show resistance** (e.g. to confinement) and refusal to cooperate when he does not like something
- Plays "peek-a-boo, patty-cake"
- **Waves** "bye-bye"
- Music now produces different types of **body movements** (similar to dancing)
- Able to scrub his body with soap and use a toothbrush
- May invent a type of hiding game (e.g. hides behind the bed cover or pulls it about his head and waiting for you ask "where are you?")

2.3 Cognitive Development

Your ten-month-old now understands the meaning of the word "no", but may not always follow. He may begin testing your limits by defying your orders intentionally.

As mentioned earlier, your child may test your limits; however he is still interested in pleasing the parents / caregivers.

Along with understanding the meaning of the word "no", your baby also understands many other words and phrases. The memory of the ten-month-old improves and fear usually comes along with the development of cognitive skills.

At this age, you may notice how your baby's intelligence is developing with the sense of perspective improving, understanding objects at a distance, expectations (e.g. knows food is on the way and he must be patient, etc), and so forth.

You may also notice that at this stage places and objects are more interesting than people are. For example, your baby will open drawers to check its contents and is interested in placing objects in there as well. Your baby is aware of himself and the environment or surroundings.

2.4 Speech & Language
- Able to say "mama, dada" indiscriminately
- May possibly be able to exchange gestures back and forth with you
- Able to imitate animal voices
- Understands few words and phrases
- Uses gibberish in a conversational manner
- May even be able to respond to a one-step command with gestures (e.g. "give that to me" with the hand out)

2.5 Self-Help and Adaptive Skills
- Starts to help when you dress him; may lift up his leg upon request or push his hands through a shirt
- Likes to still take a shower in the bath and even tries to dry his skin by himself
- Drinks from a cup

2.6 General Developmental Aspects

FEEDING
- Breast milk and/or formula and solid foods will provide the essential nutrients your ten-month-old requires.
- It is important to remember not to replace formula or breast milk with other foods as it is the basis of other foods in your baby's diet.
- Use a cup, if you have not used one already.
- Your baby may pick up and feed himself bite-size pieces of solid table foods.
- Include calcium-rich foods such as cereal, cheese, yogurt, etc.
- Some of your baby's protein may come from solids such as meat.
- Your baby may draw back the tongue in anticipation of feeding.
- Your baby may even be able to drink from a cup independently.

SLEEP
- There are no significant changes this month with sleep, however your baby may have difficulty going from a waking state to a sleeping state. In such cases, help your baby relax by holding and soothing him, giving him a bath, or even playing soft music in the background.
- Place your baby in the bed before he is totally asleep (needs to have the memory that he must go to sleep when placed in the bed).

Is Shoeless Cool?
There is no need for footwear at the ten-month-old age, even though he is newly mobile. Most doctors actually recommend no shoes at all at this age. Your baby's feet best develop when they are bare, because it helps build the arches and strengthens the ankle. If you are looking for protection when your baby is outdoors, choose low-cut baby shoes with flexible soles and uppers, flat non-skid bottoms and a roomy fit.

3. ENHANCING DEVELOPMENT

Help enhance development by:
- Repeat words your child states in adult language. Reinforce the correct pronunciation and avoid the tendency to use baby talk.
- Engage in conversations with your baby. You may notice some words or gestures that you understand.
- Play games with your baby such as "patty-cake" or "ring-around-the-rosey".
- A good way to help your baby overcome his fear of strangers is to take him with you shopping.
- Encourage your baby to crawl up the stairs, but make sure you are following close behind. Do the same thing on the way back down the stairs and help your baby place his knees and feet in the proper position for the trip back down.

TIP: Walking or Jogging with a Baby

Although walking or jogging with your baby may sound like a great bonding opportunity, keep in mind that the bouncing and jarring of motions during jogging could injure your baby's head or back. This could place your baby at risk if you fall or run into someone.

Development: 11 Months

1. GENERAL

2. DEVELOPMENTAL MILESTONES

2.1 PHYSICAL DEVELOPMENT

2.2 SOCIO-EMOTIONAL DEVELOPMENT

2.3 COGNITIVE DEVELOPMENT

2.4 SPEECH AND LANGUAGE DEVELOPMENT

2.5 GENERAL DEVELOPMENT

3. ENHANCING DEVELOPMENT

1. GENERAL

In the eleventh month of life, your baby needs your support since she is becoming her own person. Your baby is asserting her independence (e.g. solo standing, stopping, squatting, etc) among siblings and family members and begins to engage in parallel play (playing alongside but not with other children). Pointing continues to be a favorite activity and it is one way your child communicates without words. You may also notice that your baby purposely drops objects for someone else to pick up! However, while she is increasingly becoming independent, she needs to know that you are always there for her. When your baby approaches you, offer her a hug. Remember, you are not going to spoil her!

Moreover, it is common for the baby to experience steady or slow growth. If your baby was larger than average at birth, then she is probably now starting to move closer to the more genetically predisposed size.

> **Ain't Nothing High Enough!!**
> A major preoccupation of the 11th month old child is getting into things he should not be. No shelf is too high and the mission is to always destroy. Nothing will stop your baby from his target. In any confining situation, your baby will try to get out of it. As such, be sure to always supervise your child.

2. DEVELOPMENTAL MILESTONES

2.1 PHYSICAL DEVELOPMENT

The following outline the gross and fine motor skill development of the 11-month-old child. Gross motor skills refer to the ways your child uses large muscles (e.g. hands, arms, trunk, and legs), while fine motor skills refer to the ways your child uses his small muscles (e.g. dress, play, writing, etc).

Gross Motor Skills	<ul><li>Cruises while holding onto furniture (sometimes forgetting to hold on); tries climbing furniture</li><li>Able to bend forward when lying on supporting furniture</li><li>Tries to stand on one leg or tiptoes</li><li>Easily able to pull himself up to stand; bends and looks between his legs (curious to see the "reverse" side of the world)</li><li>Able to go to a sitting position from a standing position without falling</li><li>Tries to lay his weight on one hand; attempts bending and lifting toys</li><li>Climbs stairs, squats and stoops</li><li>First steps</li></ul>

Fine Motor Skills	<ul><li>Turns pages in a book (not necessarily one by one)</li><li>Can place a toy on top of the other with intent</li><li>Holds small objects in a "finer" way</li><li>Able to bring a spoon to the mouth</li><li>Able to remove the cover of a box</li><li>Can open a shoelace and remove socks off the feet</li></ul>

TIP: First Steps...
When your baby takes her first steps, you may notice that the feet tend to turn inside or inwards. It is usually self-limited and will improve or correct when the baby learns to balance her weight and her feet muscles get stronger.

2.2 Socio-Emotional Development

Socio-emotional development refers to how babies feel about themselves, their interactions with others (e.g. family, friends, teachers) and how they respond to the feelings of others.
- Does **not always** enjoy participating in groups or with others; may not always be cooperative
- May show feelings of **guilt** at wrongdoings
- Looks and waits for **permission** to do things; **seeks approval** and tries to **avoid disapproval**
- **Repeats praised actions** for more praise
- **Imitates** the movements of older children and adults
- **Enjoys games** such as "peek-a-boo" or rolling balls back and forth
- **Cries** for specific reasons
- Expresses **frustration** when something is not to the child's liking
- Increasingly **sensitive** to parents moods or others feelings
- Begins to engage in **parallel play** (playing with several things at once)

2.3 Cognitive Development

Cognitive development refers to the ways in which your child thinks and processes information (e.g. learning, understanding, reasoning, problem solving, memory, etc).

The 11-month-old baby learns a lot at this stage about **shapes, sizes and the differences between toys and other objects**. He learns that small toys go inside larger toys and that he may need to turn a cube to be able to place the smaller toy in the bigger toy. If a toy is hidden somewhere, your child will enjoy looking for it.

At this age, your baby will try to **learn the best way to solve problems**. You may help when solving problems, but try to let him do it on his own. Also, your child will attempt to use various objects and toys to achieve his own purpose. For example, he may try to use a small chair as a walker.

Moreover, **understanding words and gestures** such as "give it to me" improves during the eleventh month of life. Your child may be able to follow simple, one-step directions such as "bring the ball" or "pick up the spoon", etc. Imitating words, gestures and facial expressions become a constant mode of communication for your baby. A constant observation of your actions and the child's response is a principle-learning tool at this stage.

2.4 Speech and Language Development

Sometimes, you will feel like your baby is not hearing some of the things you are saying. This is usually because he is concentrated on a specific task and that is why he is simply not responding to you. However, have your doctor do a hearing test if you have any doubts about your child's hearing.

The 11-month-old:
- Identifies words like signs (e.g. when hearing an airplane, your child will look at the sky)
- Speaks partially clear with sounds
- Able to imitate words and actions, tone of speech, facial expressions, etc.
- Increased language skills (e.g. number of words understood, etc)
- Points to familiar pictures

2.5 General Developmental Aspects

SLEEP	• Some babies will nap only once in the day for one hour, but will sleep longer at night. • Many babies like to have naptime in the late morning hours, but then it is hard for them to go through the whole afternoon without getting tired.
TEETH	• At this time, babies may have the tendency to pull into their ears when the teeth first erupt. • If the pulling is associated with other signs (e.g. fever, sensitive ear to touch, pain, ear discharge, etc), then consult your child's doctor.
FEEDING	• Breast milk/formula and solids provide the essential nutrients at this age. • You may introduce more table foods in your baby's diet. • Babies are able to eat with their fingers, so give your baby bite-size pieces. • Do all you can to encourage your baby to eat by himself, sometimes with your help. • Mealtime may be messy, so be prepared for it. • Your baby may decide that he only like specific foods. Know that eating patterns do change and the best way to get him to eat at this age is to go with his preferences.

3. ENHANCING DEVELOPMENT

Some ways you can help your child enhance development at 11 months:

- To increase your child's range of successful cruising, show her how to reach with her arm from one piece of furniture to the other.
- Show her how to make marks on paper with crayons.
- **Create safe spaces** at home and ensure that there is enough space for your child to make distant moves without crashing into furniture.
- Develop a bedtime routine at a set time every night.
- Allow him to **explore** and have fun with toys.
- Allow him to flip light switches on and off, press elevator buttons, etc.
- Make **various facial and silly expressions** and watch your child imitate you.
- Ask your child to point to objects in picture books.
- **Read books** to her when snuggling up with a few age-appropriate stories before nap or bedtime. This will help both of you relax and strengthen your bond.
- Provide your child with large peg boards, cloth or board blocks, toys that move, large crayons and paper, different shaped toys, blocks for stacking, etc.
- **Talk often** to your child, Use simple words and labels to identify every part of her life. For example, point to trees, flowers, etc., and name objects in the bedrooms and toys in the closet. Identify and name colors, introduce concepts by describing them as big or small, empty or full, etc.
- Do not always put words in her mouth. This allows your child to answer you, either verbally or with gestures.
- **Listen patiently** to your child and respond appropriately and courteously.
- Reassure your child that she is safe by saying things like "it is ok" or "I am here".
- It is time to start setting limits. Set certain boundaries and start teaching your child the distinctions of right/wrong, safe/unsafe, etc. Remember that when she seems to be defiant, know that it is her natural inability to see how the world works.
- **Be firm and consistent** when disciplining your child. For example, say "no" firmly; take your baby away from the source of inappropriate behavior (e.g. turning off the television); and learn how to deal with a temper tantrum.

> **TIP: Baby Games**
> - **Itsy-bitsy Spider**: Repetitive music and songs (like the "Itsy-bitsy Spider") are good for infants since it allows focus on specific sounds. When syllables are broken down, it is easier to notice and pick up on.
> - **This Little Piggy**: Games that involve touch (like "This Little Piggy") are great ways to help your child learn the physical nature of the world.
> - **Peek-a-boo:** Games that demand mutual involvement (like "Peek-a-boo" or "Hide-and-Seek") encourage infant hand-eye coordination.

Development: 12 Months

1. GENERAL

2. DEVELOPMENTAL MILESTONES

2.1 PHYSICAL DEVELOPMENT

2.2 SOCIO EMOTIONAL DEVELOPMENT

2.3 SPEECH & LANGUAGE

2.4 COGNITIVE DEVELOPMENT

2.5 SELF-HELP ADAPTIVE SKILLS

2.6 VISION

2.7 ADDITIONAL DEVELOPMENTAL ASPECTS

3. SUCCESS! STIMULATING DEVELOPMENT

4. PARENTING: DISCIPLINE

5. DEVELOPMENTAL SCREENING & RED FLAGS

1. GENERAL

Happy Birthday! Your baby is now entering the toddler stages of child development. Often times, parents miss the small baby they held in their arms for hours on end, and cherish the early days. Now, your child's world is enlarging, bringing new excitement and challenges to you as a parent. She is now becoming ready to explore her world as she figures out how to let go of objects, pick them up again, and watch you as your patience wears thin.

Get ready! Slowly but surely, you'll begin to see behaviors and a newfound growing independence in your little tot. The first year of life brings with it numerous special milestones!

TIP: When your baby begins to take her first steps and falls, a quick hug and a few relaxing words can help her try again. If your response is delayed, she may begin crying due to a feeling of failure rather than physical trauma. Gradually, your baby will learn the walking process completely.

FIRST STEPS: Feet Direction
When your baby takes her first steps, her feet will turn outward because of weak hip ligaments. During the first six months of the second year of life, ligaments will tighten and the feet should then be pointed nearly straight.

2. DEVELOPMENTAL MILESTONES

2.1 Physical Development

About 60% of babies walk around their first birthdays. Despite the fact that babies are able to stand on their own at this time, some babies are not yet ready to take the first step. Most babies (75%) walk by the time they reach 13 ½ months of age, and some, even later. The following is a summary of your baby's physical development for one year of age:

ARMS & LEGS

- Shows a combination of standing, walking and cruising (*crawling is still easier than walking since it is a means of faster locomotion*)
- Able to walk and hold onto furniture (cruising)
- Able to climb and leaves the crib or playpen
- Stands alone momentarily (many achieve this by 13 months)
- Pushes toys with hands and arms (becoming a favorite hobby)
- Walks forward or sideways with one or both hands held

Able to stand & walk alone

BODY

- Sits easily for indefinite periods of time
- Able to rise from a sitting position and from a lying down position without assistance
- Able to pull herself up to stand

Trying to rise from a sitting position

Baby sits indefinitely for long periods of time

HANDS

- Tries to place toys in the mouth
- Places objects into and out of containers
- Spends minutes trying to turn off light switches and other buttons
- Walks forwards or sideways with one or both hands held
- Claps hands and waves bye-bye; raises arms to be picked up
- Scribbles, turns 2-3 book pages at one time
- Able to pick up objects neatly with the tips of the thumb and forefinger (most will achieve this by 15 months)

2.2 SOCIO EMOTIONAL DEVELOPMENT

The one-year-old:

- Expresses emotions (affection, anger, joy, fear)
- Shows affection to familiar and favored toys
- Reacts to strangers, strange places and separation from the mother
- Shy or anxious when faced with strangers or people that are not often seen
- Uses few gestures and facial expressions to get needs met
- Listens with pleasure to music, sounds, etc.
- Begins to show interest in pictures
- Understands simple requests, questions (e.g. no, do not touch)
- Sense of humor is developing (e.g. she is satisfied if she did something that made you laugh and she will try to do it again to elicit the same response)
- More alert of good and bad behavior

> **TIP: Separation Anxiety**
> • Your child may be distressed when you leave, as she experiences separation anxiety. Help your child feel more independent by not hovering over her all the time. In addition, the following are some tips to help ease the departure:
> • Ask the babysitter or caregiver to arrive early, so that your baby will have time to adjust.
> • Act in a matter-of-fact manner when you leave.
> • Do not prolong the agony with an extended or long goodbye – *just leave*! Be sure to make the departure quick with one kiss goodbye.

2.3 SPEECH & LANGUAGE
Speech and language skills in the one-year old include:
- Vocalization contains mostly vowels and many consonants;
- Says "DADA" and "MAMA"
- Turns immediately to own name
- Understands several words (e.g. cup, spoon, ball)
- Attention span may be 2-5 minutes
- Engages in gibberish conversations; babbles with inflections
- Tries to imitate words and talk "with" you

2.4 COGNITIVE DEVELOPMENT
The one-year-old child will now **explore objects in many different ways** (e.g. stacking, banging, dropping). She will be able to **find hidden objects** easily and begins to **use objects correctly** (e.g. drinking from a cup, using a brush for the hair). In addition, your child will look at the correct picture when an **image is named, copies sounds** and actions of others and tries to **accomplish simple goals.** Between the ages of 12-24 months, she will be **able to point** to one body part, **match** named objects, and **stack** about 3 blocks when asked.

2.5 SELF-HELP ADAPTIVE SKILLS
Ranging from 10-16 months, your child will begin learning to **dress herself**. Between 12-18 months, your child will be **spoon-fed**. She is able to **eat by herself, drinks** from a cup independently and use a spoon.

2.6 Vision
- Looks in the correct places for toys that are hidden or roll out of sight
- Watches small toys being pulled along the floor or across the room by about 10 feet
- Watches the movements of people, animals, and others
- Recognizes familiar faces from 20 feet or more

Parent Concern
How do I know if my child has vision problems?
✓ Your child may be experiencing vision problems when you notice frequent eye rubbing or squinting. In the older child, he may complain of headaches while reading, sits too close to the television, struggles to read or remain on task.
✓ **Warning signs of a vision in children up to 1 year**:
➢ Babies older than 3 months of age should be able to follow or "track" an object (e.g. toys, balls) with their eyes as it moves across their field of vision.
➢ Babies older than 4 months of age occasionally cross their eyes. However, eyes that cross all the time or one eye that turns out is usually abnormal; consult your child's health professional.
✓ **Warning signs of vision in the preschool child**:
➢ If the child's eye becomes misaligned (strabismus), then consult your child's health professional right away.
➢ Problems such as lazy eye (amblyopia) may present no warning signs and the child may not complain of any vision problems.
✓ **Warning signs of vision problems at any age**:
➢ Eyes that look crossed, turn out or do not focus together
➢ Any changes in eyes from how they usually look
➢ White, grayish white or yellow color material in the pupil
➢ Eyes that flutter quickly from side to side or up and down
➢ Eyes that are always sensitive to light
➢ Bulging eyes
➢ Persistent eye itchiness or infection
➢ Redness in the eyes that does not go away
➢ Droopy eyelids
➢ Excessive rubbing or squinting of eyes
RED FLAGS THAT TODDLERS HAVE VISION PROBLEMS:
✓ Tilts the head to see better
✓ Seems to tear excessively
✓ Closes one eye to see better
✓ Seems overly sensitive to light
✓ Red eyes that do not go away within a few days
✓ Seems especially clumsy
✓ Presents persistent unusual spots in the eyes in photos
✓ Droopy eyelids

2.7 Additional Developmental Aspects

FEEDING

- During the first year of life, a child's appetite decreases and growth rate is slower than the first year. Do not interpret this normal decrease in eating as a sign of illness and disease.
- Never force eating. He will decide when and how much to eat.
- Baby foods are still accepted; most babies at this age are eating table foods.
- Discuss with your doctor about weaning to whole cow's milk (if so, limit the amount to 16 ounces a day).
- Offer a spoon when eating, even though many do not achieve utensil feeding until around 18 months of age.
- Ensure that he eats with the family and is included in mealtime discussion.
- Offer your child 3 meals per day with a mid-morning and mid-afternoon snack.
- Avoid foods that pose choking risks (e.g. popcorn, peanuts, hot dogs, carrot or celery sticks, grapes, corn, hard candy, raw vegetables)
- Do not get into the habit of substituting, bribing or begging your child to eat. Your child will determine the amount of food needed. Never over-load her plate.

ORAL

- Start brushing teeth with a pea-sized amount of toothpaste.
- Your child should not fall asleep with a bottle in the mouth.
- Consult with your doctor regarding your child's first dental visit.

SLEEP

- Children often resist going to sleep at this age, because they want to be around people, objects and new environments.
- Most babies will still require the one nap a day, while others do not need to sleep at all. There is no rule for nap duration.
- Encourage your baby to console herself, and place her in bed awake.
- Some children still experience nightmares. Comfort your child for a short period of time, until you feel everything is okay.
- If your child wakes up during the night, do not offer a bottle to fall her back asleep. This will only reinforce night awakenings.

> **SAFETY**
>
> - One year of age is the minimum age for riding in a car seat that is faced forward.
> - Do not leave your child unsupervised in a bathtub or swimming pool, even if she is wearing floating accessories.
> - Ensure that any harmful or dangerous substances are out of reach and all cupboards (especially the one under the sink) are locked.
> - Now is the time to safety check and baby-proof your house, if it is not already done. Here are some extra pointers to watch out for:
>   - No slippery carpets in an area of play
>   - Furniture should be strong and without any damaged or risky areas
>   - No large boxes with toys inside that she can empty out and step inside to lock herself
>   - No sharp corners

3. SUCCESS! STIMULATING DEVELOPMENT

Walking – Encourage locomotion!

- **Pushing a toy** can help steady a child who is insecure or unclear when standing or walking.
- Let your child push a chair, a large box or a basket.
- Let her walk along the couch.
- Ensure that there is enough **safe space** for her to practice walking indoors and/or outdoors.
- Place intriguing objects out of reach to provide her with incentives for pulling and/or cruising.
- Pulling and pushing toys is great practice for those who just started walking.
- **Riding toys** may help children propel with their feet.
- If your baby seems to be inactive, you may need to crawl yourself to challenge her to crawl or walk after you by playing "catch me if you can".
- Physically show her how to move, walk, stand, and sit up when she is experiencing difficulties.

Solving Own Problems: Let Your Child Play Sherlock Holmes!

It is important to let your child solve her own problems. Do not let your impatience cause you to interfere any more than necessary. For example, you may be tempted to feed your child to help end the feeding session quicker; do not interfere in your child learning a valuable skill of feeding herself.

Toys – Time for fun!

1) **Dexterity toys**: These require twisting, turning, pressing, pulling, etc., to encourage children to use their hands in a variety of ways, after parental demonstration.
2) **Shape-shorter toys**: This means placing parts of toys inside an opening of a similar shape. Babies may need many demonstrations before they are able to master a shape shorter.
3) **Bath toys** for water play allow the joy of play in the water and promote development (e.g. filling and tipping water from a container).
4) **Musical toys** are a great way of teaching your child different sounds.

> **TIP: Toy Safety** - Be sure that toys are not small enough to cause a choking hazard

Creative Materials

-**Books and magazines** are great to show your baby. Show the same book several times, as she will enjoy the familiarity of the books (helpful for developing language skills). These materials are wonderful for building a foundation for reading.

- Allow your child to hold a book and turn the pages.
- Make sounds (e.g. animal noises) and name pictures when reading.
- Try books with one large picture on each page and help your child learn to identify the name of the picture.

-Allow your child to **scribble with crayons**, when supervised.

> **APPLAUSE!** Cheer for your baby when a new skill is mastered. Self-satisfaction is important.

Conversation – Talk to me!

a) Talk in a simple language with short sentences.
b) Name an object held out in front of your child.
c) Wait for your child to respond with a word, gesture or sound.
d) Take your child for walks outdoors and ask her what she sees or hears.

4. PARENTING & DISCIPLINE

One-year-old children have **impulse control issues**, regardless of their intelligence and/or advancement. They will want to touch, taste, smell, etc., everything in the surrounding environment. While this is important developmentally and should not be discouraged, you must watch for **safety issues and set boundaries**. These will lay the foundation for future discipline.

Not to mention, they have short memory spans. As such, time out at this age is harsh punishment without any effective results. Your child may very well forget what she is in a time out for by the time the time out is up. Rather, **explain to your child as simply as possible that "no" means that behavior is not acceptable**. Reserve serious discipline for dangerous situations (e.g. electrical cord playing). Explain this in a **stern** manner and repeat it whenever the action is present, as many times as required. Maintain eye contact when stating "no", as it is almost always effective at this age.

Learning not to do something is a major first step towards self-control. The better your child learns the lesson now, the less you will have to intervene in years to come.

The following are some examples of what you can do:

- **Distraction** can effectively deal with undesirable behaviors.
- **Direct** your child to something she is allowed to play with.
- **Consistency** is critical, so ensure that everyone agrees on what is allowed and not allowed for your child.
- **Immediacy** is also incredibly important. React as soon as you see your baby heading into a dangerous or unacceptable situation.
- **Respond** to good behavior with hugs, kisses, praise, etc.
- Do **not hover** over your child all the time. Allow her to feel independent, while knowing that you are around and dependable.
- **Do not force** your baby to interact with strangers.
- Begin teaching your child **manners** since she is receptive at this age. Emphasize words like "please" and "thank you". It is never too early to start!
- Help your child **make connections** between objects and names (e.g. count stairs as you climb them, point out the name of colors on fruits/veggies, name familiar objects, ask your child if she wants to put on red or blue socks, etc). Simply keep asking – you may be surprised!

> **TIP: Kicking & Biting**
> If your child kicks, bites, or grabs another child, take her to the side and explain that what she did was wrong and is not acceptable. Then, help her begin a new activity. Be prepared to have this conversation often and begin to teach your child what is allowed and what is not allowed (see sections on *hitting* and *biting* for further information).

Setting Limits & Limiting Settings
- Part of your child's job is to explore and discover new things in her environment. However, this can sometimes lead to dangerous situations. *Consistency in setting limits is a crucial part of parenting*; ultimately, keeping your child safe.
- Your child must learn that the outside world can be hazardous and she must learn what objects and situations to avoid.
- Moreover, setting limits teaches your child the skills to interact respectfully with others.

Instead of simply telling your child what she cannot do in a situation, try to direct your child to the alternative – the safer and acceptable way. You may offer more than one activity so that your child may feel like she is in control of the situation.

5. DEVELOPMENTAL SCREENING & RED FLAGS

It is important to review and repeat developmental screenings at every age of your child's life in order to assess progression, regression, or any difficulties. Developmental skills are to be mastered by the appropriate age in 85-90% of children. Although each child is unique, some children have not yet mastered a skill due to various contributing factors such as developmental problems, lack of opportunity to learn or practice, cultural norms, parent/child interaction, environmental limitations or prematurity (i.e. premature infants may develop later than their peers). Review the following developmental screening to assess your child's development. If you check one or more "no" responses or a *red flag* is present, then discuss with your child's health professional.

PHYSICAL DEVELOPMENT

Gross Motor Skills:
- Walks with help (holding on hands or furniture pieces)
- Gets up into a sitting position without help
- Pulls up to stand on furniture
- Stands alone and may take a few steps

Fine Motor Skills:
- Picks up small items using thumbs and first finger (fine pincer grasp)
- Turns the pages of a book (a few at a time)
- Removes objects from containers or lids to find toys
- Points at objects
- Scribbles on paper with crayons
- Able to bang 2 objects together

YES	NO

SOCIO-EMOTIONAL DEVELOPMENT

- Plays social games like patty-cake and peek-a-boo
- Shows emotions (fear, joy, affection, mad, happy, sad)
- Attracts attention by using various gestures (sounds, points, extends hands to show you)
- Indicates wants by pointing or gestures
- Seeks comfort (e.g. reaches to be held when upset)

YES	NO

COGNITIVE DEVELOPMENT

- Looks for hidden objects, remembering its last placement and finds it
- Looks at the correct picture when image is named
- Looks across the room to a toy when adults point it out
- Expresses needs and protests by using facial expressions and sounds
- More alert to good and bad behaviour

YES	NO

SPEECH AND LANGUAGE

Receptive Skills:
- Understands and follows simple requests (no, do not touch, sit down)
- Recognizes names of familiar objects
- Responds to "no"
- Listens when spoken to

Expressive Skills:
- Offers one-word responses with meaning or uses 3-5 words (even when inaccurate) – needs not be clear
- Uses gestures and facial expressions to communicate (waves hi and bye, shakes head)
- Combines sounds together as though talking (e.g. 'aba-daba-doo)

YES	NO

SELF-HELP ADAPTIVE SKILLS

- Helps when being dressed (e.g. extends arms to put in sleeves)
- Likes to undress by herself
- Lifts cups to mouth and drinks with 2 hands
- Eats finger foods

YES	NO

For the following "Definite Red Flags", consult you child health professional, if one or more of your answers is "yes".

DEFINITE RED FLAGS

	YES	NO
Loss of any previously obtained skills in any developmental domain		
No response when own name is called		
No single words are uttered		
Does not exchange sounds back and forth with you		
More interested in looking at objects than people's faces		
Fails to establish eye contact or maintain contact with you		
Rarely engages socially (e.g. eye contact, smiling, etc)		
Does not smile, gesture or point to meet needs		
Social games are not enjoyable (patty-cake, peek-a-boo)		
Cannot stand when supported		
Difficulties swallowing foods or eating solid foods		
Child can't hear/tunes out		

Please note that developmental screening checklists are not 100% or case sensitive. As such, always consult with your child's health professional regarding any developmental concerns.

Parent Concern

If my baby goes bare foot, will this cause flat feet?
Going barefoot is probably the best for children at this age, since it allows their feet to develop naturally. There is no evidence that feet develop differently with or without shoes. Shoes are there to protect your child from cuts, injuries, etc.

When does my child become a toddler?
Stages are determined by what happens to a child mentally, socially, and intellectually. An infant becomes a toddler at the age of one. The toddler stage occurs between the ages of one and two and continues until about 3-4 years. Some characteristics of a toddler include: mobility is increasingly ore noticeable, independence becomes identified, defiance is normal, mimics behavior of those around him/her, faces become less round and arms and legs are more defined, thinks she is the center of everything and often grumpy when she is forced to do things she doesn't want to do or like to do, touches and gets into everything, begins to suffer from separation, begins to develop a strong sense of self, and easily upsets.

Development: 18 Months

1. GENERAL

2. DEVELOPMENTAL MILESTONES

2.1 PHYSICAL DEVELOPMENT

2.2 HEARING & SPEECH

2.3 SOCIAL BEHAVIOUR & PLAY

2.4 COGNITIVE DEVELOPMENT

2.5 SELF HELP & ADAPTIVE SKILLS

2.6 ADDITIONAL DEVELOPMENTAL ASPECTS

3. ENHANCING DEVELOPMENT & PARENTING

4. DEVELOPMENTAL SCREENING & RED FLAGS

1. GENERAL

Your 18-month old toddler is full of boundless energy and curiosity. You can expect your toddler to become more vocal. He is typically known as 'Mr. No'! While he seems to understand the concept of 'no', he is unable to control numerous impulses. With the newly found independence, the ability to walk allows separation, yet the child continues to be very dependent and need secure attachment to the parent. Your toddler is exploring the environment around him and this is certainly a fun time! Enjoy this month in your toddler's life along with him!

2. DEVELOPMENTAL MILESTONES

2.1 Physical Development

The following are gross motor skills of physical development for the 18-month old child:

ARMS
- No longer needs to hold upper arms in extension for balance
- Likes to pull, push, and throw things (e.g. pushes large toys, boxes, pulls off hats, socks, and mittens)
- Carries large dolls or teddy bears (sometimes two of them) while walking

---

TRUNK & BACK
- Backs into small chairs or slides in sideways to seat himself
- Creeps backwards downstairs or occasionally bumps down a few steps on buttocks, facing forwards

---

LEGS
- Walk on feet only slightly apart, usually without help
- Runs carefully with head erect, eye fixed on the ground about 1-2 yards ahead
- Climbs forward into adult chairs, turns around and sits
- Walks up & down stairs (often up with a helping hand)
- Kneels upright on a flat surface without support
- Flexes knees and hips in squatting positions to pick up toys from the floor and usually rises with helping hands
- Able to kick a ball around

> **Fine motor development** entails the movement part of development, specifically of small muscle use. To perform fine motor skills, appropriate vision is needed.

- Picks up small beads, pins, and threads with delicate pincer grasp motions
- Builds towers of three cubes after someone demonstrates (sometimes occurs spontaneously)
- Turns pages, sometimes several at a time
- Points to distant interesting objects, usually outdoors
- Begins to show preference for using one hand
- Imitates a crayon shake on paper
- Tries putting on his own shoes
- Scribbles with crayon
- Holds spoon and gets food safely into the mouth
- Holds cups between both hands; lifts cups alone but usually hands it back to adult when finished

VISION

- Able to fixate on mounted balls at ten feet to 1/8 of an inch, however attention is easily distracted
- Fixed eyes on small dangling toys at ten feet
- Recognizes himself in the mirror

2.2 Hearing and Speech

- Understands many words, but does not grasp abstract concepts (at this age, toddlers are strictly concrete thinkers)
- Uses 6-20 or more recognizable words and understands many more
- Vocabulary increases to 50 + words between the ages of 18 months - 2 years
- May combine 2-word phrases
- Enjoys nursery rhymes and tries to join in & attempts singing
- Obeys simple instructions (e.g. "shut the door")
- Names familiar objects correctly (e.g. hair, nose, feet, toys, etc)

2.3 Social Behaviour & Play

At the age of 18 months, children **explore** their environments energetically and with increasing understanding. Toddlers at this age can now briefly **imitate** simple, everyday activities (e.g. feeding dolls and reading books), as well as imitating others (e.g. talking on the phone or vacuuming). Increasingly, toddlers show **affection** by kissing parents and exhibiting various emotions including fear, sympathy, happiness, modesty, guilt, and embarrassment. However, separation from close family members and friends continue to produce some **anxiety**. The concept of sharing has yet to be developed. Also, the 18 month-old:

- Remembers where objects belong & returns them to their rightful place when finished playing
- Shows increased interest in playing with other children
- Likely to be afraid of separation from close family members & friends
- Enjoys playing with adults, especially playing repetitive games or alone on the floor with toys
- May be cooperative in dressing due to a desire to copy and "do it myself" attitude

- Directs another's attention to an object or action
- Seeks attention and seems selfish at times
- Protests when frustrated; all children will experience tantrums, reflecting their inability to delay gratification, suppress or displace anger or verbally communicate their emotional status.

2.4 COGNITIVE DEVELOPMENT

Toddlers develop **understanding, sensory and thinking skills** at this age. They now can point to some body parts directly as well as familiar objects when known, imitating behaviors and uses toys appropriately. Playing is more likely to now be used for their intended purposes (e.g. car for driving or cup for drinking).

The concepts of time, distance and speech are beyond child's grasp at this age. Yet, the **ability to remember**, copy and paste events (i.e. improving memory) is developing, along with the **ability to work out which objects go together** (e.g. crayons and paper), completing simple **puzzles,** enjoying simple **make-believe** (e.g. pretending to talk to someone on the phone or pretending to drink from an empty cup), as well as the **understanding of size and space** (e.g. scared to slip down the plug hole in the cup).

Finally, the 18-month-old toddler is able to **communicate his wishes** and intentions. He is beginning the **imitative and symbiotic use of toys** by identifying objects in a picture book, laughing at silly actions (e.g. wearing a bowl on the head), looking for objects that are out of sight, following 1-step directions and solving problems by trial and error.

2.5 SELF-HELP AND ADAPTIVE SKILLS

- Use of cup (open/Sippy cup) at 15 months (range 10 -18 months)
- Imitate house work – 18 months (14-24 months)
- Use words or gestures indicating need to go to bathroom
- Pushes arms through sleeves, legs through pants
- Eats table food with spoon independently

2.6 ADDITIONAL DEVELOPMENTAL ASPECTS

FEEDING

- During the toddler years, your baby's appetite decreases and caloric needs are down; this is normal since your child probably did not grow much recently either.
- Allow your child to drink with a cup and feed himself since he is able to do it pretty well.
- If your child refuses to eat, do not make a "big deal" out of it; mealtime should not be a battle.
- Avoid using excessive snacks in between meals.
- Share meals whenever possible and make mealtime pleasant.
- Avoid using foods as reward or punishment.

TOILET TRAINING

- Some children will show readiness for toilet training between 18-24 months. Readiness for dryness can be manifested by (a) the child reporting wet or soiled the diaper; (b) long periods of dryness; and (c) ability to pull pants up and down.
- Let your child watch family members use the toilet.
- If he is not ready to start training, do not push him.

ORAL HEALTH

- Do not put your child to bed with a bottle.
- Brush your child's teeth with a pea-size amount of toothpaste.

SLEEP

- Encourage consoling himself by putting him in bed awake.
- Your toddler may start to give up one nap. For some, one nap is not enough while for others it can be too many.
- If night awakening, night terrors, etc., occurs, discuss this with your doctor.

SAFETY
- Supervise whenever he is outside, going up or down the stairs, in the bath, pool, etc
- Always apply sunscreen.
- Place home detectors in your home (e.g. smoke, carbon monoxide)
- Make electrical wires and tools, medicine and so forth, inaccessible in your home.
- Always place car restraints when your child is in the car.

3. ENHANCING DEVELOPMENT & PARENTING

To enhance development, you can:
a) **Play ball** with your child. Allow him to kick, throw, and catch the ball.
b) Allow him to make use of body in various movements (e.g. running, climbing, swinging, jumping, etc).
c) **Dance** with him by playing fun music and show him how to move his arms in a swaying motion, march to the music, hop and clap his hands.
d) **Provide toys** that he can pull and push together (e.g. containers with lids, Lego toys).
e) **Draw and color** using large crayons and talk about what you are drawing together.
f) Offer him simple puzzles to play with.
g) **Help notice familiar sounds and objects** (e.g. dogs barking, sirens).
h) **Play games** and provide opportunity to say "no" (e.g. Is Daddy under the bed?").
i) Set up **play-groups** for your child and play-groups.
j) **Imitate noises** you hear and see if your child imitates you.
k) Show what he can do and use simple, one-step directions.
l) **Read** stories.
m) **Enhance communication**: Toddlers understand more than they can say so TALK, TALK, and TALK! Provide opportunities for him to speak with you.

n) Enhancing memory: Babies think that what they cannot see has disappeared; however toddlers have an idea of object permanence (i.e. the object is still there even if he does not see it). They are developing a working memory, so you can help enhance your child's understanding of object permanence and memory by referring to past or future events with key words such as yesterday, today or tomorrow.

PARENTING

- Match toys to your child's age that do not contain any small pieces that may pose as choking hazards.
- Allow your child to learn how to entertain himself.
- Teach your child simple songs that are easy to learn.
- Divert his attention from things he should not do.
- Keep rules to a minimum without any long or heavy speeches; "because I said so" should be enough for now.
- Remember to be firm and consistent, but loving and supporting at the same time when disciplining your child.
- Encourage your child to make his own choices whenever possible.
- Show affection and encourage an environment that allows for open and free emotional expression.
- Praise and encourage good behavior and accomplishments.

4. DEVELOPMENTAL SCREENING & RED FLAGS

It is important to review and repeat developmental screenings at every age of your child's life in order to assess progression, regression, or any difficulties. Developmental skills are to be mastered by the appropriate age in 85-90% of children. Although each child is unique, some children have not yet mastered a skill due to various contributing factors such as developmental problems, lack of opportunity to learn or practice, cultural norms, parent/child interaction, environmental limitations or prematurity (i.e. premature infants may develop later than their peers). Review the following developmental screening to assess your child's development. If you check one or more "no" responses or a *red flag* is present, then discuss with your child's health professional.

NOTE: If your child falls between two age groups, use the earlier developmental screening (e.g. a 23-month old child will be reviewed with the 18-month old checklist). **Sometimes, babies have not been trained/taught to complete certain tasks such as identifying pictures in a book or asked to point to objects. In such cases, when all other aspects of the screening are fine, then you need to teach the child then follow and reassess. In any case, discuss with your child's health professional.**

Please note that developmental screening checklists are not 100% or case sensitive. As such, always consult with your child's health professional regarding any developmental concerns.

PHYSICAL DEVELOPMENT

Gross Motor Skills:

- Walking alone/backwards
- Walking up the stairs with or without assistance
- Pulls and pushes toys/objects while walking
- Squats to pick up toys without falling

Fine Motor Skills:

- Holds and drinks from a cup
- Brings the spoon to mouth in an attempt to feed himself
- Picks up and eats finger foods
- Stacks 2 blocks of objects
- Scribbles

YES	NO

YES	NO

SOCIO-EMOTIONAL DEVELOPMENT

- Demonstrates some type of pretend play with toys
- Enjoys being read to and sharing simple books with you
- Looks at you when you are talking or playing together
- Exhibits negative feelings (e.g. stubborn, upset, independent)
- Exhibits a full range of emotions (e.g. happy, sad, angry)
- Communicates needs with gestures (e.g. directs parent), and with words

YES	NO

SPEECH, LANGUAGE AND COMMUNICATION

Expressive Skills:

- Uses at least 6-30 words or more, even if the words are not clear
- Points to show you something
- Makes at least 4 different consonant sounds (e.g. p, s, m)
- Points to familiar pictures using one finger

Receptive Skills:

- Points to at least 2 different body parts when asked
- Responds with words or gestures to simple questions

YES	NO

SELF-HELP ADAPTIVE SKILLS

	YES	NO

- Takes off his own socks, hats with help
- Takes off his own socks, hats without help
- Helps in dressing by sticking out his arms and legs for you
- Tries to take off his own shoes

DEFINITE RED FLAGS

	YES	NO

- Loss of any previously obtained skills in any developmental domain
- Plays with toys in unusual ways (e.g. lining up, spinning, opening and closing parts rather than using the toys as a whole)
- Preoccupied with unusual interests (e.g. switches, doors, fans)
- Does not listen when others are talking to him
- Unable o point to objects when they are named
- Not showing any preference for familiar people but more to objects
- Does not show any awareness for different people
- Rarely engages socially (e.g. smiling, eye contact)
- Unusual quality of voice
- Out of control, hyperactive, and uncommunicative
- Passive, withdrawn, demanding and stubborn
- Not yet walking
- Difficulty eating solids or swallowing
- Persistent rocking, hand flapping, head banging, and toe banging

For *"Definite Red Flags"*, consult your child health professional, if any answer "yes"
COMMENTS: 18 Months of age is one of the recommended ages to do developmental screens for autism. Please see chapter on recognition of symptoms of autism. Remember that the child who was born prematurely often lags behind others of the same chronological age. This developmental gap progressively narrows and generally disappears around the age of 2 years.

Development: 2 Years

1. **GENERAL**
2. **NORMAL DEVELOPMENTAL MILESTONES**
   - *2.1 PHYSICAL DEVELOPMENT & VISION*
   - *2.2 COGNITIVE DEVELOPMENT*
   - *2.3 LANGUAGE, HEARING & SPEECH*
   - *2.4 SOCIO-EMOTIONAL DEVELOPMENT*
   - *2.5 SELF-HELP ADAPTIVE SKILLS*
3. **BEHAVIORAL DEVELOPMENT: DISCIPLINE AND OTHER PARENTING ASPECTS**
4. **ENHANCING DEVELOPMENT**
5. **ADDITIONAL DEVELOPMENTAL ASPECTS**
6. **DEVELOPMENTAL CHECKLIST & RED FLAGS**

1. GENERAL

By two years, your child is no longer a baby, but "*Miss Independent*". She will assert her independence at mealtimes, bedtimes and even during attempts at toilet training. While she is now able to run, feed herself, state a few words, and move things, she is still a baby in many ways. She may not know what she wants exactly but, surely it is not what you want and as such, she may be difficult and if not impossible at times. At this stage, reasoning with may be difficult. Toward the end of this year, she may join a playgroup and start to play with other children in a constructive way. Still lovable and fun, this year, your child may even surprise you with a burgeoning imagination!

2. DEVELOPMENTAL MILESTONES
2.1 PHYSICAL DEVELOPMENT & VISION

ARMS
- Opens doors, puts on hats & shoes
- Carries large toys while walking
- Pulls toys behind the body while walking
- Pushes and pulls large, wheeled toys easily
- Throws small balls forward without falling

HANDS
- Scribbles spontaneously/ turns containers over to pour contents
- Builds towers of blocks of 4 or more
- May use one hand more frequently than the other
- Can wash and dry hands/ uses a spoon and cup well
- Picks up pins & threading accurately, quickly and places them down neatly with increasing skill
- Holds a pencil in the preferred hand and uses the thumb & the first two fingers
- Imitates vertical lines and sometimes the "V" shape

LEGS
- Walks alone
- Begins to run safely-starting & stopping with ease
- Stands on tiptoes
- Kicks balls
- Climbs onto & down from furniture unassisted
- Walks up and down the stairs with support or climbs up steps alone with step at a time, holding the stair railing or parent's hand
- Jumps on the floor with both feet
- Squats with complete steadiness to rest or play with objects on the ground and rises to feet without using any hands
- Sits on a small tricycle, but cannot use pedals (propels the tricycle forwards with feet on the floor)

VISION
- Enjoys picture books & recognizes fine details
- Recognizes familial adults in photographs after being shown once but not the self as yet

2.2 Cognitive Development

By two years of age, your child:
- Begins to **sort** by shape and colors
- Begins **make-believe play**
- Finds objects, even if they are hidden under 2-3 covers
- **Asks** frequent questions (e.g. what is that?)
- Selects and **uses toys appropriately** (e.g. feeding dolls, hammers pegs into a bench)
- **Categorizes** faces, animals and bird according to their individual characteristics
- Names pictures of familiar objects
- Looks for new ways to work toys
- **Puts together** simple puzzles
- Shows a **basic sense** of time when told "later" or "soon" or "not now"
- **Understands consequences** of physical actions (e.g. pushing a button will turn the light on)

2.3 LANGUAGE, HEARING, AND SPEECH

Receptive Language	Expressive Language
Points to objects when named	States several single words (by 15-18 months)
Recognizes names of familial people, objects and body parts	Uses single phrases (by 18-24 months)
Follows simple instructions	Often experiences short periods of mild speech abnormalities (e.g. stuttering)
Understands many words (usually 50 recognizable words)	Repeats words heard in conversations
Begins to listen with obvious interest to general talk	Refers to self by name; talks to self continuously in long monologues while playing (yet much is still incomprehensible)

TIP: Vocabulary
Most 2 year olds have a vocabulary of 50 or more words. This number varies with: the sex of the child (girls tend to speak more than boys), siblings (that may speak with/to the child), or if two languages are spoken in the house. Child vocabulary escalates from 10-15 words to 50-200 words by 2 years. After acquiring a vocabulary of about 50 words, toddlers begin to combine them to make simple sentences - the beginning of grammar.

2.4 SOCIO-EMOTIONAL DEVELOPMENT

SOCIAL DEVELOPMENT
Your child will express **increasing independence** and begin to demonstrate **defiant behavior**, however she will continue to experience **separation anxiety** (especially during the middle of the second year of life) – this will fade with time. She will now easily **imitate behaviors** and activities by others, especially those of older children and adults. She will spontaneously engage in simple role or situational make-believe activities, **constantly demanding** the **attention** of others. Moreover, she is increasingly aware of oneself as a separate person, and becomes **increasingly enthusiastic** about the company of other children. The two-year-old child is intensively **curious** about the environment and her surroundings.

EMOTIONAL DEVELOPMENT
The two-year-old displays a wide range of emotions and behaviors such as love, pleasure, joy and anger. They also tend to protest a lot. When interacting with others, they explore various new activities and will want to do things for themselves.

INTELLECTUAL DEVELOPMENT
Children can form images in their minds, make judgments, and categorize (e.g. dogs and cats are animals; cups and plates are dishes). They can arrange things in order (e.g. lining up bricks by size) and by this point; their memories are much more sophisticated as they are beginning to understand more abstract concepts (such as "more" versus "less", "later" versus "sooner"). The imaginations of two-year-old children are more fertile, allowing their play to be more creative.

2.5 SELF-HELP ADAPTIVE SKILLS

- Uses spoon and cup well
- Opens doors
- Puts on hats and shoes
- Can wash and dry hands

TIP: Curiosity of Body Parts
Do not worry if your child becomes curious about body parts - it is normal at this stage. Teach and use the correct terms for body parts including genitals.

3. BEHAVIOURAL DEVELOPMENT: DISCIPLINE & OTHER PARENTING ASPECTS
3.1 DISCIPLINE

Discipline is incredibly important at the two-year-old stage of life. The word *discipline* means 'to teach', and so discipline can become a learning experience for both you and your child. The following are some helpful tips on how to discipline the two-year-old child:

- Any form of discipline should be **firm** and consistent, yet **loving** and understanding at the same time
- **Do not** try to reason or argue with your child, especially with **long speeches** or explanations - they are completely useless. Simply state "*because I said so*" should be enough for now. As your child grows, explanations will be more useful and needed
- **Avoid power struggles** since no one wins.
- **Do not shout or spank**, rather use the two "I's" of discipline: isolate and/or ignore. Always try to make a **verbal separation** between the child and the behavior (e.g. "I love you, but I don't like it when you touch the television")
- **Praise** when she achieves developmental milestones of any kind (behavioral, social, or emotional)

Some other tips to disciplining include:

- **Encourage** her to make her **own choices** whenever possible. However, these should be limited to those you can handle (e.g. red or green socks, blue or red shirt).
- **Provide alternatives.** For example, offer a different toy if your child is playing with something you do not want her to play with.
- **Never ask an open-ended question**, unless you are ready to accept the answer (e.g. would you like to take a bath?)

3.2 PARENTING

The following are some helpful hints on how to parent the two-year-old child in accordance with discipline.

Arrange **safe times** for running and exploring the outdoors.

Let her interact with other children to allow her to experience playing with peers. This can certainly be accomplished in a playschool or **having a play-date** for a few hours.

Limit the viewing of television and do not use it as a baby sitter or substitute for interaction. Watch with her whenever possible and be sure the television is turned off during mealtimes.

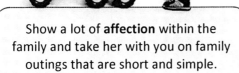

Spend time teaching her how to play and encourage **imaginative play** and **toy sharing** (do not expect sharing at this age yet).

Show a lot of **affection** within the family and take her with you on family outings that are short and simple.

4. ENHANCING DEVELOPMENT

The following outlines various ways to help enhance your baby's development:

1. **Provide toys** that have pedals so that she learns to use her feet to move. Help her climb on and off the toy and teach her how to pedal using her feet. Praise the effort she makes.
2. Allow her to safely **practice climbing and jumping** (e.g. jumping from a bottom step).

3. Give an old purse full of "cool" objects inside. Allow her to **pull everything out** and place it back inside. This is good practice for teaching how to clean and place objects where they belong.
4. Allow her to **open and close** containers by twisting and turning the lids. Place all the lids and containers in front of her and allow her to find the right sized lid to place on the proper container.
5. **Sing** animal songs (e.g. "Old MacDonald's") and show her how to maneuver like an animal (e.g. hop like a frog, jump like a bunny, or quack like a duck)
6. **Provide words for her feelings** and show that you understand so that she may learn about emotions.
7. The perfect "let's pretend" game is **dress-up** and this can be played at any age. Use any old clothes, shoes, purses and hats as ideal items for a dress-up box (it is much more fun to play with these than special child-size outfits from the store).
8. **Play together** in fun activities like in the sandbox and show her how to use buckets and pails. You can also teach how to properly play in the sandbox (e.g. not throwing the sand).
9. Sing songs and repeat them. **Leave out some parts of the song for her to fill** in. This is great for intellectual development.
10. **Painting and coloring** is a great way to learn about colors and textures.
11. Jigsaw puzzles demand concentration; dexterity and visual understanding so provide fun puzzles. If she gives up quickly, then provide her with an easier puzzle to start off with.
12. Play various games that include **sorting objects** by shape, touch, colors and size. Use spoons, blocks, toys and clothing. You may try the shoebox game where you use two shoeboxes and two toys, taking turns placing the toys under, over, beneath, behind, and on top. Explain these actions while performing them.
13. **Help her learn new words** by talking to during bath-time, feedings or dressing. Name clothing, body parts and anything and everything else (e.g. sorting the laundry, set the table, and when you place groceries away).
14. **Use picture books** to enrich your child's vocabulary, as reading books will help her language development.
15. Your child wants to become independent at this age, so **encourage her to do things on her own** (e.g. getting dressed and undressed, doing household tasks, and opening and closing doors).

HELPFUL HINT: Imagination
Do not waste money on expensive kits and toys that promise early creativity. A big cardboard box is enough for your child's imagination to build a house, car, boat, etc.

5. GENERAL DEVELOPMENT

Other general developmental aspects are:

SLEEP
- An afternoon nap is still required by most two-year-olds.
- Children should sleep in their own beds
- Some sleep problems can occur at this age, including refusal to go to bed, getting out of bed and wandering around the house at night, nightmares and night terrors.
- "Stalling techniques" are common at bed and naptime such as the child stating that he has to go to the "potty" or wants a drink.
- Bedtime is a good time to read a story to your child.

TOILET TRAINING
- Signs of toilet readiness include the following:
  - *Awakening from a nap with a dry diaper*
  - *Having bowel movements at the same time everyday*
  - *Being able to say "wee-wee" or "poo-poo"*
  - *Knowing when she has to go*
  - *Being able to take off her own clothes*
  - *Do not try to over-train your child since this can delay the process, making the child nervous and tense. Do not make it a battle.*
- If your child has bowel movements at the same time everyday, you may seat her on the potty chair and "catch it". A favorable response from you sends the right message
- If bowel movements occur at irregular times in the day, then watch for a characteristic expression and position that indicates a bowel movement. When this occurs, pick her up and place her on the potty. If nothing happens within a few minutes, take her off the potty.

- When your child has an "accident", stay calm and do not punish her. If you act distressed or angry when your child fails, training may be delayed.
- Praise accomplishments and let her know that you are pleased.
- Note that by being pushy, irritated or scolding your child, you are delaying her development of voluntary control and laying the groundwork for a "toilet problem".

SAFETY
- Use proper car safety restraints in the backseat of any car trip.
- Beware of chewed up or picked at old painted surfaces.
- Watch out for any items that can be left at counter level such as knives, scissors, cleaning products or household repair items
- Never place poisonous substances in food containers or bottles.
- Keep any firearms locked away and out of sight.
- Gate any pools.
- Ensure that she is wearing a life vest on a boat.
- Use waterproof sunscreen before going outside (around 10 am – 3 pm) when the sun is most dangerous.
- Never leave her unattended in the bath, car, or house
- Be careful of what you place in the wastebasket.
- Watch if she is playing on the street at all times.
- Make sure the smoke detector in your home is working properly.

> **TIP: Head Circumference**
> 90% of adult head circumference is achieved by age 2 years with just an additional 5cm gain over the next 5 years.

FEEDING
- Your child does not grow much at this age and as such she may not consume food as much as you would expect
- Appetite is finicky and varies from day to day and meal to meal. Let your child's appetite be your guide and let her choose what foods to eat.
- Do not expect three good meals per day.
- She can tell her likes and dislikes and will frequently want the same food item, day in and day out.
- Milk may change to 2% milk, if approved by your child's doctor.
- Discuss vitamins and fluoride supplements with your child's doctor.
- Family meals are important, so allow her to feel like she is part of the family by helping out and sitting with the family.
- Make sure your child's caregiver is following feeding instructions.

ORAL HEALTH
- Check your child's oral health with your dentist.
- When she sees you brushing your teeth, take advantage of this and show her how to do it too with her own toothbrush.
- It is okay to use small amounts of fluoridated toothpaste.

6. DEVELOPMENTAL CHECKLIST & RED FLAGS

It is important to review and repeat developmental screenings at every age of your child's life in order to assess progression, regression, or any difficulties. Developmental skills are expected to be mastered by the appropriate age in 85-90% of children. Although each child is unique, some children have not yet mastered a skill due to various contributing factors such as developmental problems, lack of opportunity to learn or practice, cultural norms, parent/child interaction, environmental limitations or prematurity (i.e. premature infants may develop later than their peers). Review the following developmental screening to assess your child's development. If you check one or more "no" responses or a *red flag* is present, then discuss with your child's health professional.

NOTE: If your child falls between 2 age groups, use the earlier developmental screening (e.g. a 2 ½ year old child will be reviewed with the 2 year checklist).

PHYSICAL DEVELOPMENT

Gross Motor Skills:
- Walks by 18 months of age
- Walks up and down the stairs without help
- Walks to the side or backwards when pulling toys
- Carries large toys while walking
- Throws and kicks small balls forward
- Begins to run safely (starting and stopping easily)
- Climbs onto and down from furniture without help
- Plays in a squat position

Fine Motor Skills:
- Holds books the right way up or turns pages one at a time
- Scribbles with crayons on papers
- Stacks 4 blocks
- Eats food with utensils independently, spilling a little

SPEECH, LANGUAGE AND COMMUNICATION

Receptive Skills:

	YES	NO
Follows simple instructions or 2-step directions		
Responds when name is called		
Can answer simple questions		
Identify body parts		

Expressive Skills:

	YES	NO
Forms words or sounds easily		
Uses 2-word sentences by the age of two		
Uses at least 2 pronouns (e.g. "you, me, mine")		
Words are understood most of the time (about 60%)		

SOCIO-EMOTIONAL DEVELOPMENT

	YES	NO
Enjoys being around or playing with other children		
Shows pretend play patterns e.g. tea party, feeding doll		
Imitates adult functions e.g. wiping tabletop, phone use		
Shows affection		
Expresses independence in word and action e.g. says "No" and has temper tantrums		

COGNITIVE DEVELOPMENT

	YES	NO
Seems to know the function of common household items (e.g. phone, fork)		
Points to familiar objects when asked (e.g. ball, hat)		
Makes scribbles and dots on paper		
Recognizes the use of familiar objects		
Finds objects even if they are hidden under 2-3 covers		
Understands consequences of physical actions (e.g. pull switch and light turns on)		
Points to 6 body parts		
Uses gestures or words for assistance (e.g. waves hands at you to be held)		

SELF-HELP ADAPTIVE SKILLS

	YES	NO

- Can undress himself with one article of clothing
- Eats food with spoon independently, spilling a little
- Takes off own shoes, socks, or hat
- Opens doors and puts on hats and shoes
- Uses spoon and cup well

For the following "Definite Red Flags", consult your child health professional. If one or more of your answers is "yes".

DEFINITE RED FLAGS

	YES	NO

- No response when name is called
- Experiences a dramatic loss of skills
- More interested in objects than people
- Preoccupied with unusual objects (e.g. light switches, parts of toys)
- Cannot undress himself with one article of clothing
- Talks in "scripts" from TV shows or books (i.e. in his own world)
- Echoes others words
- Does not put together 2-word combinations
- Does not scribble (e.g. neuro-developmental disorders)
- Lack of interest in toys or plays with them in unusual ways e.g. lining up, spinning, opening-closing parts, rather than using the toy as a whole

Please note that developmental screening checklists are not 100% or case sensitive. As such, always consult with your child's health professional regarding any developmental concerns.

TIP: Blocks Constructions – An Age and Number Guide
9 Months = Holds 1 block in each hand
18 Months = Constructs 3 blocks
2 Years = Constructs 6-7 blocks
2 ½ Years = Constructs 7 blocks
3 Years = 9-10 blocks
4 Years = More than 10

Additional Comments: Emotional Development
- At this age, children develop the ability to recognize themselves in the mirror (which may be necessary for developing the emotions pride, shame, embarrassment and guilt).
- Children at this age also develop prosocial behaviors including sharing, cooperation, and helping behaviors along with the emotions empathy and sympathy, which require that the child can identify the emotions of others.
- It is important for parents to display affection and sensitivity towards their child in order to foster empathy.
- Children also become better at self-soothing and regulating their emotions.
- The more synchrony that exists between parent and child, the stronger the emotional bond between them.

Development: 3 Years

1. **GENERAL**
2. **DEVELOPMENTAL MILESTONES**
   2.1 PHYSICAL DEVELOPMENT: GROSS MOTOR SKILLS
   2.2 PHYSICAL DEVELOPMENT: FINE MOTOR MOVEMENTS
   2.3 COGNITIVE DEVELOPMENT
   2.4 SPEECH & LANGUAGE DEVELOPMENT
   2.5 SOCIAL BEHAVIOUR & PLAY
   2.6 SELF-HELP ADAPTIVE SKILLS
   2.7 ADDITIONAL DEVELOPMENTAL ASPECTS
3. **DISCIPLINE**
4. **ENHANCING DEVELOPMENT**
5. **DEVELOPMENTAL SCREENING & RED FLAGS**

1. GENERAL

The third year of life should be much easier on you as a parent, since many three-year-olds enjoy doing things for themselves. At this age, many toddlers ask numerous questions about anything and everything as they are experiencing their surroundings in a new and independent light. At the same time, most toddlers have an incredible amount of energy and enjoy interacting with other three-year-olds, learning and developing their social skills. Thus, allow your child to enjoy toddler time by providing the space required for your child to run, climb, pull toys, ride tricycles, etc. Many toddlers continue to use security objects such as a favorite blanket or stuffed toy. It is perfectly normal to hold on to that security favorite; they will give it up when they are ready.

2. DEVELOPMENTAL MILESTONES

2.1 Physical Development: Gross Motor Skills

Your 3 year old is now able to:

Walks up the stairs alone with alternating feet

Walks down the stairs two feet at a time
Climbs any nursery apparatus with agility
Rides tricycle
Runs easily (sometimes quickly)
Able to kick, throw, & catch large balls

Able to stand & walk on tip toes; able to stand on one foot briefly

Jumps in place

Pushes & pulls large toys around

TIP: Handedness
Handedness is usually established by the third year of life. Frustration may result from attempts to change children's preference (see further on *Handedness*).

2.2 PHYSICAL DEVELOPMENT: FINE MOTOR MOVEMENTS

The following are some of the finer movements of physical development. Proper vision capabilities are also necessary to appropriately perform these fine motor movements.

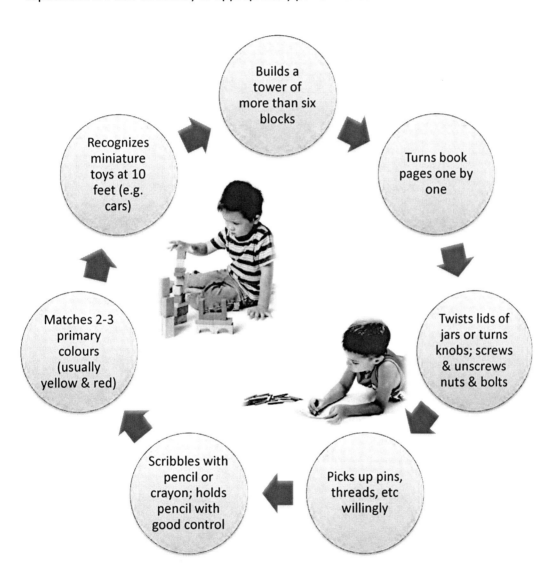

2.3 Cognitive Development

The mental capability of a child at the toddler stage is still tied to the concrete and physical. They are not yet aware of concepts such as change over time and its meaning. At times, your child may be confused between facts and fantasy. However, most three-year-olds can be reasoned with.

Your 3-year old child is able to:

- ✓ Identifies common objects & pictures
- ✓ Follows commands with parents request some of the time
- ✓ Cooperates with parents request some of the time
- ✓ Listens to music or stories for 5-10 minutes
- ✓ Matches objects to pictures in a book
- ✓ Able to make mechanical toys work
- ✓ Completes puzzles of 3-4 pieces
- ✓ Sorts objects by shape and color
- ✓ Understands concepts of two or two-step directions (e.g. pick up your toy and place it on the table)
- ✓ Able to draw a person
- ✓ Builds blocks with the intent of building towers and trains, etc.
- ✓ Understands the use of some words such as "out, in front of, under, over, big, dirty", etc
- ✓ Enjoys showing new knowledge learned
- ✓ Makes inferences about new members of a category

2.4 Speech & Language Development

- More than 50% of children's speech is **intelligible**. However, there may be temporary episodes of **stuttering** during this time.
- Your three-year-old child will **ask many questions** such as what, where and why. He will **listen** eagerly to stories (even demanding favorites) and **understand** most sentences read or stated to him. He probably knows several nurseries rhymes and sometimes, even songs.
- Personal pronouns (e.g. "I, you, they, me, we") are used correctly, along with plurals and most prepositions. **Two to five word sentences** are uttered at this age such as "I go home now". Family and strangers can clearly understand most of the child's words.
- Speech continues to show many **unconventional grammatical forms**. However, your child will be able to **provide his full name and sex**, sometimes age as well.
- He will still **talk to himself in long monologues** that are mostly concerned with immediate presence, including make-believe activities.
- Your toddler will carry on **simple conversations** and will briefly be able to describe present activities and past experiences.

> **TIP: Temper Tantrums**
> Tantrums usually appear towards the end of the first year of life and peak in prevalence between 2-4 years of age. If tantrums last for more than 15 minutes or occur regularly (more than 3 times/day), or persist beyond 4 years, then discuss this with your child's health professional in order to rule out any underlying medical, emotional, or social problems your child may have.

2.5 Social Behavior & Play

Play increases in complexity and imagination from simple imitations of common experiences (e.g. shopping and putting a baby to bed; at 2-3 years of age) to more extended scenarios involving singular events such as going to the zoo or going on a trip (at 3-4 years of age); and, to the creation of scenarios that have only been imagined such as flying to the moon (at the age of 4-5 years).

> Affectionate & confiding; Expresses a wide range of emotion including showing affection for younger siblings; Enjoys floor play with boxes, toy trains, dolls or with siblings

Likes to help adults in domestic activities (e.g. gardening, shopping, etc); Objects to major changes in routines; Separates easily from parents

Makes an effort to keep surroundings tidy; Understands sharing play objects; Imitates adults and playmates (may be helpful – e.g. putting toys away)

Plays make-believe or imagination games with actions & words (e.g. dress-up as mom or dad); Joins in active make-believe play with other children; Dry through the night (but very variable)

2.6 SELF-HELP ADAPTIVE SKILLS
- Able to dress himself (still requires help putting on shoes and with fastening or buttons)
- Able to open doors
- Eats with a fork and spoon
- Stabs food with fork and brings food to the mouth
- Brushes teeth
- Dries hands without help when given a towel
- Washes hands and face using soap

2.7 ADDITIONAL DEVELOPMENTAL ASPECTS

EATING HABITS
"My child won't eat" is a common complaint of parents of three-year-old children. Some of the things you can do to help improve your child's eating habits include:

- Limit juice and sweet foods intake
- Stop pacifier use
- Allow your child to feed himself
- Eat dinner as a family (whenever possible)
- Offer exciting meals (e.g. finger foods, dips, food shapes, etc)
- Remember to watch out for food choking hazards such as nuts, hard candies, hot dogs, etc.

TIP: For further details about toddler eating habits and how to improve these habits, you can refer to the book *Feeding and Nutritional Health for Babies and Toddlers* or *visit our website:* www.babyandtoddlerhealth.com.

SLEEPING HABITS

New things (e.g. nightmares, fears) may interfere in your toddlers sleeping habits. The following are a few pointers to improve your toddler's sleeping habits:
- An afternoon nap is usually still required at this age.
- It is important to maintain a consistent bedtime routine.
- Fear of the dark is a common concern at this age. In order to lessen this fear, place a night light in your child's room and let your child know that you are just "a room away".
- Nightmares may wake up your child from a sound sleep. Reassure your toddler and place him back in bed.

SAFETY MEASURES
Begin teaching your child their full name, phone number and address.

- Explain to your child that he should not talk to strangers.
- Advise your three-year-old to be careful around strange animals (e.g. dogs).
- Watch your child when he is playing close to the street (at this age, toddlers do not understand its associated dangers). Never leave your child unsupervised or unattended to in a car or in a house.
- Ensure your home is smoke-free with smoke and carbon monoxide detectors.
- Any swimming pools in or outside of the home should be gated.
- Continue to use proper car safety restraints in the back seat of every car trip.

NOTE: If one has a trampoline in the home, then it should be kept away from the young child. Trampolines are not recommended due to the risk of serious injury.

TOILET TRAINING
- Many three-year-olds are trained for during the day, but are still not dry at night, while others are completely trained.
- Avoid placing too many demands on your child or showing him weaning diapers. Instead, let your child know how proud and happy you are about any potty or toilet success.
- Note that some children postpone having a bowel movement as a way of manipulation against the parents or simply because they are doing something else.

Try not to make an issue of this; your child will be successfully toilet trained with your encouragement and support.

3. DISCIPLINE

- Discipline should be **firm and consistent**, yet loving and understanding when disciplining a three-year-old child. Never forget to constantly **praise and encourage** your child for good behavior and accomplishments.
- Shouting and/or spanking are never a "good" way of disciplining your child. Rather, **ignore or isolate** your child when trying to discipline; try separating the child and his behavior. For example, say something along the lines of "I love you but I don't like when you touch the computer".
- **Providing alternatives** is always an excellent way of averting inappropriate behavior to appropriate behavior. For example, you can tell your child that while he is not allowed to touch the computer, he is allowed to play with the song piano book.
- Always **avoid power struggles**, because no one ever wins! Don't forget that three-year-olds still use temper tantrums as a weapon and you should be prepared to deal with this behavior by responding with ignorance or isolation (e.g. time-outs).

- **Never make threats that you cannot carry out**. If you are going to say you are doing something, then be sure to do it!

4. ENHANCING DEVELOPMENT

HELPFUL HINTS TO ENHANCE DEVELOPMENT FOR THE 3 YEAR OLD:

a. Continue reading various types of books to your child.
b. Arrange safe times for running and exploring the world outdoors.
c. Plan play dates and social gatherings for your child and peers in his age group.
d. Limit the amount of television your child views. Do not use the television as a babysitter or as a substitute for interaction with other children. Whenever possible, watch a children's program with your child.
e. As your child becomes curious about the body, use the correct and proper terms for genitals. Children at this age begin to recognize gender differences between girls and boys.

f. Keep family outings short and simple, as children have short attention spans at this age. Lengthy and/or complicated activities may become tiring and irritable.
g. Encourage your child to do things on his own to become more independent and learn responsibility (e.g. dressing/undressing, helping to clean up, washing himself, etc).
h. Help your child feel safe, especially when he seems to have a particular fear (e.g. afraid of the dark, afraid of small animals)
i. Encourage your child to play puzzles, blocks, and build Lego's or trains. Invite him to enjoy intellectually stimulating games.
j. Talk with your child and let him know that it is okay to ask questions and answer them as truthfully as possibly.
k. Model phrases such as "please, thank you, and sorry" so that your child may imitate you.
l. Take your child to the playground. Do not restrict playground use simply because your child never wants to leave the playground. Distract him with something exciting to get him away from the playground when it is time to leave (e.g. "Let's go see Daddy!").

FUN GAMES!

Let's Play Ball! Encourage your child to throw and catch balls. You can add other props such as a toy or plastic bat or plastic gloves to help throw and catch the ball.

Play the Line! Place a rope on the floor (tape it with masking tape) and have fun with your child, jumping, running, standing, galloping over the line, etc.

Make-Believe Time! Go camping, dancing, fishing, and have tea parties with your child. **Sorting Fun!** Allow your child to sort objects by shapes or colors (e.g. sorting beads, buttons).

Guess What? Hide objects in a bag and allow your child to feel the bag and smell the bag so that he can guess what it is and then pull it out to see if he got it right.

5. DEVELOPMENTAL SCREENING & RED FLAGS

It is important to review and repeat developmental screenings at every age of your child's life in order to assess progression, regression, or any difficulties. Developmental skills are expected to be mastered by the appropriate age in 85-90% of children. Although each child is unique, some children have not yet mastered a skill due to various contributing factors such as developmental problems, lack of opportunity to learn or practice, cultural norms, parent/child interaction, environmental limitations or prematurity (i.e. premature infants may develop later than their peers). Review the following developmental screening to assess your child's development. If you check one or more "no" responses or a *red flag* is present, then discuss with your child's health professional.

NOTE: If your child falls between 2 age groups, use the earlier developmental screening (e.g. a 3 ½ year old child will be reviewed with the 3 year checklist).

PHYSICAL DEVELOPMENT

Gross Motor Skills:

- Walks up the stairs using handrail
- Stands on one foot briefly
- Throws a ball forward (at least 3 feet) or over hands
- Gets up from a squatting position without help
- Rides on an tricycle using pedals (needs practice)

Fine Motor Skills:

- Builds blocks of more than 4
- Twists lids off jars or turns knobs
- Copies a circle and imitates vertical lines

YES	NO

COGNITIVE DEVELOPMENT

- Understands 2-step directions (e.g. "take the book and bring it to me")
- Understands & uses some descriptive words (e.g. big, small)
- Understands who, what, where, when and why questions
- Names 1-3 colors
- Completes an easy puzzle of 4-6 pieces
- Names 4 pictures by animals or objects

YES	NO

SPEECH, LANGUAGE AND COMMUNICATION

Receptive Skills:
- Understands much of what is said (pictures, colors, names)
- Can hear you when you call his name from another room
- Understands simple direction and follow 2 step commands (e.g. put the ball in the box)
- Can listen to stories and answer simple questions

Expressive Skills:
- Speaks clearly enough to be understood most of the time by familiar members and strangers
- Speaks 2-5 word sentences
- Tells simple stories, can find a song, a nursery rhyme

YES	NO

SOCIO-EMOTIONAL DEVELOPMENT

- Plays make believe or pretend games
- Shows affection with words and actions
- Plays with other children of the same age comfortably
- Joins in play with two or more children
- Talks about events
- Talks about feelings and interests
- Enjoys pretend play with roles for the self or for dolls and action figures

YES	NO

SELF-HELP ADAPTIVE SKILLS

- Dress or undress with help
- Washes and dries hands

YES	NO

For the following "Definite Red Flags", consult your child health professional, if one or more of your answers is "yes"

DEFINITE RED FLAGS	YES	NO
Loss of any previously attained social or language skills		
Lack of response to name called		
No interest or little interest in looking at people (prefers objects)		
Child is mostly in own world rather than interacting with others		
Plays with toys in an unusual manner		
Difficulty manipulating small objects		
Unable or extremely difficult separating from mother		
Fails to understand simple instructions		
No imaginative or make-believe games		
Unclear speech or unable to communicate with short phrases		
Obsession with unusual objects (e.g. doors, wheels, fan, etc)		
Echoing others words		
Prone to temper tantrums when compulsions are disturbed		
Persistent echolalia (repeating what was just said)		

Please note that developmental screening checklists are not 100% or case sensitive. As such, always consult with your child's health professional regarding any developmental concerns.

6. Parent Concerns
"Our son may be color blind. What do I do?"
- Most children cannot distinguish colors until the age of 3-4 years.
- Color blindness is typically passed from mother to child.
- It does not affect sharpness of vision or acuity at all.
- The deficiency limits the ability to distinguish between green and red, and occasionally blue.
- Variations exist in color blindness (e.g. some are able to identify strong hues, others have difficulty with lighter shades). Other children who cannot identify color due to dim lights, and others with severe color blindness see everything in shades of grey.
- Children most often confuse the following shades: pink/grey, orange/red, white/green, blue-green/grey, and yellow/brown.

- Teach color to your child by identifying and naming colors whenever you can (e.g. colors of clothing, cars, objects, etc).
- After your child masters the basic colors (red, blue, green, yellow), teach the subtler colors of pink, brown, orange, and purple. Discuss with a teacher how to help a child with color deficiency.

My 3-year old boy consistently picks and pulls out his belly button, sometimes to the point of bleeding. What should I do?

- Initially, consult with your health professional that there are no signs of infection, redness, or other causes (e.g. eczema) that cause your child to pick at his belly button. Sometimes infection results from an excess collection of dirt or moisture from precipitation (e.g. not drying after bathing). Also, itchiness may increase the risk of bacterial infections. If there is no infection and all is well at the doctor's visit, then picking one's belly button may just be a habit and aversion to it.
- You can use lotion to change the texture of the belly button to help him stop picking at it. As soon as you see your child picking his belly button, you can use a distraction method to help him stop (e.g. take his hands and place a book or a toy in them).

What should I do when a child seems to regress?

- It is not uncommon for children to go back to their old familiar patterns. It is especially true when children are ill or experiencing a family transition (e.g. moving homes, new siblings).
- The most important response is to exercise patience since this will almost certainly turn around quickly.
- To get your child back on track, you can:
  - ✓ Support him through transitions by talking, preparing and alleviating anxieties surrounding the transition.
  - ✓ Do not embarrass your child who is backsliding; it is certainly not motivating.
- If your child continues to regress with no improvements or signs of advancing, then consult your child's health professional.

Development: 4 Years

1. General

2. Developmental Milestones

2.1 Physical Development: Gross Motor Skills

2.2 Physical Development: Fine Motor Skills

2.3 Hearing & Speech

2.4 Social Behaviour & Play

2.5 Cognitive Development

2.6 Self-Help Adaptive Skills

2.7 Additional Developmental Skills

3. Enhancing Development

4. Parenting & Discipline

5. Developmental Screening & Red Flags

1. GENERAL

The four-year-old child develops more independence, self-confidence and self-reliance. They explore the environment (through play, dressing) and ask a lot of questions about relationships, sex, and different people. As your child grows, a newfound confidence is developed where she may become more boastful and "show-off" by intentionally misbehaving (especially with peers). Thus, discipline is mainly used at this stage by the constant need to pull your child aside and speak to her about the misbehavior. Do not reprimand your child publicly since she may be tempted to continue the behavior.

KINDERGARTEN: How to Ease the Transition

- Typically, children begin junior kindergarten around the age of four years.

- There are many things you can do to help ease the transition between home and school for your child.

- For starters, you can **make a plan** for the very first day your child will attend kindergarten by reviewing where you will be taking her, who you will be leaving her with, what she will be doing, when you will be picking her up, etc. This will allow for an easier morning when you take her to kindergarten by deterring a long and sad goodbye.

- Encourage her to begin the **first steps to independence**. She should feel excited, self-reliant and self-confident. You can help promote these by allowing your child to dress on her own in the morning, as well as listening to her stories at the end of the day.

- **Help expand your child's vocabulary and language skills** by paying attention to your child's words, and helping her use more advanced vocabulary.

- Take her **to play-dates and playgroups** to help advance cooperation and teamwork. This will help build social skills and make friends, which is a big part of kindergarten.

2. DEVELOPMENTAL MILESTONES

2.1 Physical Development: Gross Motor Skills

- Sits with knees crossed
- Moves backwards and forwards with agility
- Walks or runs alone
- Can stand on one foot (preferred) for 3-5 seconds and hops on the preferred foot
- Moves herself around skillfully, turning sharp corners and running
- Can stand, walk and run on tip toes
- Expert rider of the tricycle
- Goes up and down the stairs without support
- Kicks ball
- Climbs ladders

2.2 Physical Development: Fine Motor Skills

- Sits with legs crossed
- Picks up and replaces very small items (e.g. pins, thread) with each eye covered separately
- Threads small beads to make necklaces
- Builds a tower of 10 or more cubes and several bridges of three from one model, on request and spontaneously
- Holds and uses a pencil with good control (similar to adults)
- Draws recognizable homes, faces, arms and legs on request
- Copies shapes such as circles, crosses and possibly squares (usually by 5 years however)
- Able to cut with small scissors
- Arranges and picks up objects from the floor by bending down from the waist with the knees extended
- Eats skillfully with a spoon and fork
- Washes and dries hands
- Able to brush her own teeth
- Can undress and dress (except for laces, ties and buttons)
- Throws ball above the head
- Catches a bounces a ball most of the time

2.3 Hearing and Speech

The following outlines the development in hearing, language and speech of the four-year-old child:

- Great conversationalists
- Vocabulary includes about 1500 words
- Enjoys jokes
- Shows only a few infantile phonetic substitutions usually of the "r-l-w-y," "p-th-f-f" or "k-t" group
- Endlessly asking questions (why, when, how) and the meaning of words
- Provides understandable accounts of recent events & experiences
- Provides full name, home address, and usually age as well
- Knows several nursery rhymes, which she repeats and sings correctly
- Listens to and tells long stories, sometimes confusing fact from reality; able to communicate elaborate stories by stringing up to 8 words together at a time (will talk about things happen to her as well as fantasies)
- Counts up to 20 or more and begins to count objects by words and by touching (can usually count from 1-10) in correspondence up to 4-5
- Speech is grammatically correct and completely intelligible; for the most part, speech is quite clear/understandable yet the "f, v, s, z" group may still give your child trouble until midway through the 5th year (may still use some sounds correctly -e.g. say 'th', for 's' or 'w' for 'z')

2.4 SOCIAL BEHAVIOUR AND PLAY

The general behavior of the four-year-old child is characteristic of **independence** and a **strong self-will**. Most are inclined to verbal impertinence with adults (asking more questions, especially about their sexuality) and **quarreling with playmates** when wishes cross. Four-year-olds certainly show a unique sense of humor when talking and when joining in activities. They engage in dramatic  **make-believe play** (that has become more sophisticated) with dressing up as a favorite, and their ability to distinguish fact from fantasy improves. Another favorite that they can certainly achieve at this age is **constructive outdoor building** with any materials available. They require and **enjoy the regular interaction and companionship of other children** with whom they are alternately cooperative and aggressive (as with adults). Playing cooperatively and showing interest in other children's bodies, they also enjoy engaging in conversational "give & take" and can sing a variety of songs.

One of the great things about four-year olds is that they now understand that they can **argue** with other children with words rather than with blows. Moreover, four-year-old children understand the concepts of **sharing and taking turns** (at least some of the time), showing concern for younger siblings and **sympathy** for playmates in distress. Simply put, they are able to now appreciate the past, present and future.

Four-year-olds can **identify emotions** such as sadness, anger, anxiety and fear. They can also now **understand simple rules** and most obey these rules. However, friends and peers at this age begin to exert some influence over your child's behavior. Your 4-year-old may start testing your authority and challenge your limits of her independence. It is important to reprimand your child if she does not respect your rules. This is especially so since at this age, she may still have a few tantrums when she does not get what she wants.

IMAGINARY FRIENDS

Between 45-60% of children have one imaginary friend at some point. This can include a stuffed animal that children instill with distinct personality traits or an invisible imaginary companion (about 25% of children). It may look like the child has lost touch with reality or is delusional. The child may have an imaginary friend because she does not have enough real friends or lacks the social skills to make friends. In fact, some experts believe that these children tend to have more friends in school and are more socially sophisticated in general.

Typically, imaginary friends present during the preschool years and usually fade away by age 7 for unclear reasons. It is possible that these imaginary friends are present to help build social skills or they arise as a response to difficulties the child is facing (e.g. illness, family stress). Either way, parents should not necessarily worry about imaginary friends. It may be a beneficial adaptive coping mechanism, providing children with distance from an uncomfortable situation.

2.5 COGNITIVE DEVELOPMENT

The ways a child thinks and processes information is improving. As your child gets older he is:

- Learning to **sort objects** by shape, color and size and by what sort things fall into, while noting similarities and differences by animals, colors, shapes, etc.
- **Endlessly asks questions**, sometimes embarrassing or difficult to answer, such as questions about sex, death, "where babies come from", etc.
- Correctly recognizes gender differences
- Counts objects
- Able **to draw** a square and some capital letters as well as a human figure with a head, body, arms, legs and perhaps even, five fingers
- Able to name 3 coins
- Knows her age
- Knows about the season and related activities
- Knows at least 3-4 colors (may even name the colors)
- Understands concepts of "taller, smaller, shorter" (not yet able to arrange a group of things in order from smallest to biggest).
- Has a better sense of time

2.6 SELF-HELP ADAPTIVE SKILLS

Self-help adaptive skills are the day-to-day skills that are gaining in independence as your child grows. At the age of 4-5 years, children can go to the **bathroom** by themselves, using the toilet and toilet paper properly as well as being able to flush the toilet. While children are able to manage their own toilet needs during the day, they may not be able to stay dry at night. In addition, children at this age are able to **dress** on their own as long as fastenings are not too difficult (e.g. buttoning and unbuttoning, opening or closing a zipper). Further self-help adaptive skills include the following:

- Cleans up any spills by getting the cloth to clean it up with
- Washes her own face and hands
- Able to bathe herself except for her back, neck and ears
- Knows how to use the proper utensils when eating
- Able to serve herself food
- Cares for her own clothes by placing them in the proper place (i.e. closet hangers)

2.7 ADDITIONAL DEVELOPMENTAL ASPECTS

SAFETY

- Know when your child is at all times and supervise your child if she is playing close to the street.
- Ensure that there are smoke and carbon monoxide detectors in the house and that they are working properly.
- Avoid the use of trampolines due to risks of serious injury.
- Select safe toys for your child to play with.
- Keep electrical tools, matches, poisons, firearms, etc., out of your child's reach.
- Teach your toddlers not to talk to or accept foods from strangers. Some can even be taught their full names, addresses and phone numbers.
- Use a car seat or booster that secures your child properly when driving or ensure appropriate helmet use when riding a tricycle.
- Be careful when you are backing out of the driveway.
- Always make sure your child is wearing a life jacket when she is on a boat or close to any waters.
- Never leave your child unattended in a bathtub or swimming pool, even if she knows how to swim.
- Avoid placing your child in the sun during dangerous house (i.e. 10 am – 3 pm). Use sunscreen after the age of one year.
- Teach your child good habits including washing hands after using the toilet, covering one's mouth when coughing or sneezing, etc.

ORAL HEALTH
- Supervise your child brushing her teeth twice per day with a small amount of fluoridated toothpaste.
- Be sure to take your toddler to the dentist for regular check-ups and discuss any oral supplements required/necessary.
- Discourage any thumb or finger sucking. However, discuss with your dentist or health professional if your child is already thumb sucking.
- Educate yourself about what to do when your child loses a tooth or when any other dental emergencies arise.

FEEDING
- The four-year-old child will probably insist on feeding herself and imitating others in food likes and dislikes.
- Foods should never be forced onto your child; allow your child to decide what and how much to eat.
- Mealtimes should be pleasant with the provision of nutritious foods. Offer small portions with the option of adding more.
- Eat dinner meals as a family together whenever possible.
- Insist on appropriate table manners and encourage pleasant conversation during mealtimes.
- Offer snacks that are rich in carbohydrates. Limit high-fat and low nutrient foods.
- Control the amount of sweets your child eats and avoid junk foods.
- Avoid any hard candies, hot dogs, raw vegetables, and uncut grapes and so forth to avoid the risk of choking.

SLEEP
- Maintain a consistent bedtime routine by adhering to a set time your child goes to sleep, using a night light, security blanket or toy to help lessen any nighttime fears.
- Remember that nighttime fears including being afraid of the dark, thunder, etc., are quite common at this age.
- If your child does experience a nightmare that wakes her up from sleep, reassure your child and place her back in bed.

DID YOU KNOW: Toilet Training
By the age of four, 95% of children are bowel trained while 90% are toilet trained during the day and 75% are trained at night.

3. ENHANCING DEVELOPMENT
The following are some ways of how to enhance development in the four-year-old:

a) **Practice activities with your child** such as walking, running, crawling, climbing, balancing, hopping on one foot or both, and jumping over things.
b) Provide your child with opportunities to learn to ride a 2 or 3-wheeled bike with trainer wheels, to participate in outdoor physical activities.
c) Show your child how to **use sports equipment** and **how to play** (e.g. bats, soccer balls, gloves).
d) Show and encourage tying her shoes, closing buttons, and zipping up zippers.
e) **Teach** how to write the alphabet, letters, and her name and phone number.
f) Cut, paint, draw and have fun with arts and crafts.
g) **Read/tell stories** and make it fun by changing your voice for different characters and acting out different actions; explain what is happening in the pictures.
h) Allow your child to **entertain herself** by listening to books on tape.
i) Involve your child in **group games and play-dates** where simple rules are involved (e.g. games such as duck-duck goose, farmer in the dell).
j) Play **memory games** with your child using card games and toys for objects.
k) Allow your child to tell you stories by showing her pictures and see where her **imagination** takes her.
l) Allow your child to join in on your **conversations** by talking and listening to her.
m) **Hug** your child consistently and **praise** her milestones and accomplishments.

> **TIP: Dealing with Emotional Behaviour**
> Help deal with your child's anger and frustration by teaching and letting her know that it is okay to express her emotions. Encourage her to talk about any hostile feelings she has rather than acting on those feelings.

4. PARENTING & DISCIPLINE
The following are suggestions of how to parent and discipline your four-year-old child:

- Your child may be curious about body parts at this age, which is normal. Always use the correct term for genitals.
- Security objects (e.g. blankets, toys) may continue to be used. It is normal that your child will give these up when she is ready.
- Allow your child to help you in cleaning around the house, setting the table, completing chores, and so forth. Be sure to always praise your child for a job well done.
- Always praise your child for good behavior and accomplishments.

- Any form of discipline should always be firm and consistent, yet loving and supportive as well. It should be immediate, specific to the behavior and time-limited.
- Avoid shouting or panicking at your child for misbehavior. Simply ignore or isolate your child when she misbehaves or place her in a time out.
- When disciplining your child, try to separate her from the behavior. For example, you can state that you love her, but you do not like the behavior shown.
- Provide your child with clearly stated limits along with an explanation of the consequences when rules are broken. Note that time outs are usually effective punishments when done properly.
- Whenever possible, reprimand your child in private rather than in the presence of others.
- Meaningless threats are ineffective ways to punish your child. Be sure to follow through with consequences and discipline that is firm and consistent instead.

5. DEVELOPMENTAL SCREENING AND RED FLAGS

It is important to review and repeat developmental screenings at every age of your child's life in order to assess progression, regression, or any difficulties. Developmental skills are expected to be mastered by the appropriate age in 85-90% of children. Although each child is unique, some children have not yet mastered a skill due to various contributing factors such as developmental problems, lack of opportunity to learn or practice, cultural norms, parent/child interaction, environmental limitations or prematurity (i.e. premature infants may develop later than their peers). Review the following developmental screening to assess your child's development. If you check one or more "no" responses or a red flag is present, then discuss with your child's health professional.

NOTE: If your child falls between 2 age groups, use the earlier developmental screening (e.g. a 4 ½ year old child will be reviewed with the 4 year checklist).

PHYSICAL DEVELOPMENT

Gross Motor Skills:
- Go up and down the stairs alternating feet
- Rides a tricycle
- Stands on one foot for a few seconds without any support
- Hops on one or both feet
- Catches large balls with long outstretched arms

Fine Motor Skills:
- Cuts paper with small scissors
- Holds a pencil correctly (i.e. between the thumb and forefinger)
- Able to undo buttons and zippers
- Places shoes on correct feet
- Dress and undress without assistance
- Wash and dry hands without support

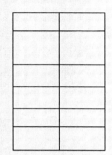

YES	NO

SPEECH, LANGUAGE AND COMMUNICATION

Receptive Skills:
- Understands most of what is said
- Understands questions and senses (e.g. what do you do with your eyes?)
- Identify color and shapes
- Follow 3 step directions (stand up, get the ball and give it to me)

Expressive Skills:
- Repeat nursery rhyme and sing songs
- Able to say some words correctly such as hat, mud, fun, key, cookie, go, now, etc
- Speak clearly so that she can be understood most of the time
- Uses sentences consisting of more than 3 words
- Uses adult type grammar
- Tells stories and makes stories from pictures shown

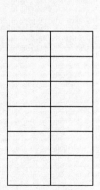

YES	NO

SOCIO-EMOTIONAL DEVELOPMENT

	YES	NO

- Share and take turns when playing with peers
- Caring and comforting when someone is distressed
- Talk or takes interest while engaging in activities with other children
- Pretend play has become more details and imaginative

COGNITIVE DEVELOPMENT

	YES	NO

- Say what to do when tired, cold, hungry (2 of 3)
- Say first name and last name when asked
- Sorts object and places them where they should be (e.g. shape, colour, animals, etc)
- Knows at least 3-4 colours and can match colours
- Understands small, tall, big, short, etc
- Recites numbers up to 20
- Recognizes some words they see a lot, such as "stop" or other road signs
- Understand 3 part directions or long sentences

SELF-HELP ADAPTIVE SKILLS

	YES	NO

- Dresses with supervision
- Eats skillfully with spoon and fork
- Able to brush own teeth
- Washes own face and hands

For the following "Definite Red Flags", consult your child health professional, if one or more of your answers is "yes".

DEFINITE RED FLAGS	YES	NO
◆ Loss of any previously attained social or language skills		
◆ Not or stopped responding when name is called		
◆ Smile and make eye contact when engaging socially		
◆ More interested in objects than people		
◆ Shows a lack of interest in toys		
◆ Plays with toys in an unusual manner		
◆ Preoccupied with unusual objects (e.g. doors, switches, etc)		
◆ Engages in fantasy and imaginative play		

Please note that developmental screening checklists are not 100% or case sensitive. As such, always consult with your child's health professional regarding any developmental concerns.

Bonding
Set aside time to bond with your child. You can participate in various activities with your child to enhance bonding.

- Bike riding
- Bedtime conversations
- Shopping
- Cooking
- Watching television
- Restaurant meals
- Going to movies
- Walking the dog
- Browsing bookstores
- Playing with toys
- Reading books
- Playing board/card games

Development: 5 Years

1. **GENERAL**
2. **DEVELOPMENTAL MILESTONES**
   - *2.1 PHYSICAL DEVELOPMENT*
   - *2.2 SPEECH AND HEARING*
   - *2.3 COGNITIVE DEVELOPMENT*
   - *2.4 SOCIO-EMOTIONAL DEVELOPMENT*
   - *2.5 SELF-HELP ADAPTIVE SKILLS*
3. **GENERAL DEVELOPMENT**
4. **ENHANCING DEVELOPMENT & PARENTING THE 5 YEAR OLD**
5. **RED FLAGS**

1. GENERAL

Five year olds are very energetic, cheerful, and enthusiastic as they are constantly seeking active environments for which they can play and release their energy. They develop increased co-ordination showing improved fine motor skills with writing. There is increased ability to balance and co-ordinate movements with speed and quality, as well as mature forms of walking, running, jumping, and so forth.

What become more fun for the parent are the endless amounts of questions your child will ask. Children at this age are beginning to look for meaning within the world. They become more aware of their behaviour and act more responsibly, decreasing aggressive behaviour and outgrowing childhood fears. At this point in their development they undergo the most dramatic growth in the brain and develop cognitive capability that allows them to become a curious creative thinker.

2. DEVELOPMENTAL MILESTONES

2.1 Physical Development

Generally, body coordination improves where the five-year-old child can skip, jump rope, hop on one foot, run on tiptoes, and learns complex body actions such as skating and riding a bicycle. The following table outlines the large muscle movements (gross motor skills) and use of smaller muscle movements (fine motor skills) a typical five year old develops.

GROSS MOTOR SKILLS	FINE MOTOR SKILLS
Able to stand on one foot for 10 seconds or longer, with arms folded	Good control of writing & drawing with pencils and paint brushes
Maintains balance while standing on one foot with eyes closed	Prints some letters spontaneously
Walks on narrow lines without stepping off; can walk backwards quickly, and runs lightly on toes	Draws a person with head, trunk, legs, arms and features (usually 6-8 body parts), as well as homes with doors, windows, roofs and chimney
Rides a bike with training wheels	Shows a clear dominance for the right or left hand

May be able to skip and on alternate feet (note that some boys lag behind in skipping as late as eight years of age depending on developmental maturation)	Copies squares, circles and triangles (usually around 5 ½ years of age) as well as capital letters
Jumps over objects and lands without falling	May produce pictures containing general items (usually indicates the background of the environment)
Hops on both feet and then one while keeping balance; climbs up and down without using the handrail; swings, slides, and digs	Names 4 primary colors and matches 10 & counts fingers on one hand with the index finger of the other hand
Begins to perform most ball-related skills (e.g. catches and throws a bouncing ball, etc)	Grips objects strongly with either hand e.g. cuts with scissors & able to cut and paste, Uses knife and fork utensils competently

VISION: Can pick up and replace minute objects when each eye is covered separately; however, still lacks eye coordination for sustained reading periods

2.2 SPEECH AND HEARING

By now, **speech is fluent** as he is able to correctly use plurals and pronouns. It is normal for there to be some **mispronunciations of some sounds** such as "s, f, v, th" – generally speaking, the speech is grammatical, conventional and usually phonetically correct. He **speaks clearly** with age-appropriate language skills with a vocabulary of **5-8 word long sentences**. He will speak to familiar children and adults, asking for the meaning of words and attempting to use these words. Also, he can provide their full name, age, birthday (usually) and home address, but also make up fun stories and retell them.

Keep in mind that children love being read to as they are able to **listen to stories** without interrupting. They are able to **ask for the meanings** of unfamiliar or abstract words to carry on in conversations. They especially **enjoy acting out these stories** to their friends later in detail. Jokes and riddles are a favorite as they are delighted when asked to recite or sing rhymes and jingles.

2.3 Cognitive Development

Cognitive development includes the thinking, understanding, and reasoning capabilities. The following points below addresses some of the basic skills your five year old has reached:

- Has a **good attention span** and can concentrate well
- Is usually able to separate fact from fantasy
- **Understands** the following**:**
    - ✓ **Cause and effect relationships** (e.g. "I don't talk to Roy because he hit me"), however does not always understand the relation between the parts to a whole
    - ✓ The **use of comparative terms** such as big, bigger, biggest or less/more/same, etc.
    - ✓ Right, wrong, fair and unfair, as well as some concepts including in/out, yes/no, front/back, before/after, etc.
    - ✓ Games that have rules
    - ✓ Better understands the concept of time (e.g. today/tomorrow/yesterday)
- Uses simple reasoning by arguing and using words such as "because"
- **Memorizes things** but does not yet have strategies (e.g. rehearsing lists)
- Can trace numbers and capital letters; may write some numbers and letters on her own (identifying some alphabet letters)
- **Identifies basic colors** like red, yellow, blue, green, and orange
- **Draws** pictures that represent animals, people and objects
- **Counts** objects (usually ten or more)
- **Sorts** similar objects by color, size and shape (e.g. animals and toys); can place objects in order from shortest to tallest or vice versa
- Looks at pictures and **tells stories**
- Able to **remember stories** and repeat them
- Follows **three step directions** and commands
- Remembers address and phone number
- Can **make comparisons** (e.g. tall/taller, short/shorter, etc)

2.4 Socio-Emotional Development

Socio-emotional development refers to the development of emotional skills (e.g. the interaction with expressing and responding to others feelings) that enable socialization and the ability to interact with others. The following points outline the socio-emotional development of the five-year-old child:

> **Plays** in the following ways:
> - Begins to **recognize rules** (e.g. makes up games with simple rules)
> - Understands the need for **organization and tidiness**, but needs constant reminders
> - Domestic play alone or with playmates (e.g. pretend play with organized children and toys); plays organized games and makes teams or assigns roles
> - Continuously plays both indoors and outdoors
> - Engages in make-believe and dress-up play (e.g. some children assume certain roles such as "mommy" or "daddy")
> - Chooses own **friends** (e.g. wants to be like his friends and wants to please friends); may exclude other children in play outside of best friends
> - **Cooperates** with friends most of the time and understands the need for fair play; cooperative play is more complex and sustained
> - Understands **sharing**, but may not always want to share
> - Able to **work independently** for a short period of time
> - **Tender and protective** towards young children and pets (e.g. comforts playmates in distress)
> - May use swear words to gain attention
> - Shows a definite **sense of humor**
> - Likes to **sing, dance and act**
> - May continue to **fear** loud noises, animals, strangers or unfamiliar faces and the dark

Five year olds can manage feelings and social situations with greater independence and use strategies (e.g. negotiation and compromising) to resolve conflicts before seeking an adults help.

- May **act bossy**, but tries new things and take risks, making their own decisions
- Able to **distinguish fantasy** from reality most of the time
- Being **accepted by playmates** is becoming more and more important
- **Interaction** with other children and adults is much enjoyed
- Gains self-esteem for feeling capable and demonstrating new skills
- Seeks and accepts adult supervision
- **Discusses feelings** and expresses emotions such as anger and jealousy

2.5 SELF-HELP: ADAPTIVE SKILLS

Your child is gaining independence at five years of age and is able to do the following day-to-day skills independently:

- **Dresses** self (laces shoes, combs hair) with little assistance and undressing continues to be easier than dressing
- Continues to perform many **self-care tasks** such as brushing teeth, hand washing, etc.
- **Serves himself** at the table and able to **feed himself** (uses forks, spoons, and sometimes, a table knife)
- Able to **work independently** for short periods of time
- Can tolerate frustrations and failures
- Able to **draw** oneself, but may not be able to draw the clothes in the correct order or facing the right way

- Toilet capabilities are in control (usually cares for **own toilet needs**), but may need occasional reminder when preoccupied
- Able to follow basic health and safety rules
- Able to respond appropriately to potentially harmful objects
- Washes and dries face and hands, but needs supervision for the rest

3. GENERAL DEVELOPMENT

SLEEP: By five years, your child should have a bedtime routine with a set time of when to go to sleep. It is normal for your child to experience the occasional nightmare or night terror.

FEEDING: Offer your child a variety of foods from the five foods groups. Limit carbohydrate intake by limiting snacks including pop drinks, chips, chocolates, candies, etc. Encourage healthy snack options (e.g. fruits & veggies) with fun dips instead. Allow your child to assist you in choosing and preparing meals for herself.

ORAL HEALTH: Your child may begin to lose baby teeth and acquire secondary teeth. At this age, you should encourage your child to brush her teeth twice a day with a small amount of fluoridated toothpaste.

SAFETY: Always make sure your child wears a seatbelt in the car. Teach your child how to swim and ensure that all swimming pools are secure and closed off from your child. Provide a smoke-free environment. Teach bicycle safety by ensuring that your child always wears a helmet. Teach your child the rules for interacting with strangers. Never allow your child to play outside unsupervised.

BLADDER AND BOWEL MOVEMENTS: Bladder and bowel control usually arise at the age of five, with girls typically toilet training sooner and faster than boys. Bed-wetting is common in girls up to 4 years of age and boys up to five years.

4. ENHANCING DEVELOPMENT & PARENTING THE 5 YEAR OLD

The following are helpful tips for how to enhance the development of your five-year-old child:

a) **Play** dress-up with your child by collecting old dresses, shoes, clothing, and sunglasses to let your child's imagination run wild.

b) Play games with your child such as hide and seek, red rover, and help your child learn the rules of the game and taking turns. You can also play board games with your child to **help him learn** better about rules, counting, taking turns, winning and losing, etc. Teach your child what is right and wrong.

c) Help your child learn how to **ride a bike** and make sure she is wearing a helmet.

d) Help your child practice **how to write and draw** with pencils and crayons. Provide him with tracing paper to copy letters and teach your child various shapes and numbers. Help him learn how to use scissors by letting her cut out with coupons.

e) Let your child **experiment** with different materials (e.g. clay, tape, scissors, papers, felt, sponges, etc) so that she can be creative.

f) **Ask** your child many questions to help improve her speech including questions like "what food is this?" and "What toy are you playing with?" Be sure to ask your child questions about their day and ask for details.

g) **Talk** to your child throughout the day about things that interest him. Listen and let your child tell you a story from beginning to end. Take your child's questions seriously and provide answers they can understand.

h) **Encourage** your child by praising him when he does something new and proper. **Praising** your child for good behavior and developmental milestones will encourage him to do it again. Specific praises will help your child understand the time value of their actions.

i) Help your child **learn** about the feelings of others through stories.

j) Observe and allow your child to **play with other children** and be part of a team and help them learn the rules. Teach your child how to request, negotiate and apologize.

k) Allow your child to pick up the phone when it rings and **help her learn** how to take a message.

l) **Read** with your child. Add drama to your reading session with different voices for the various characters and ask questions to end the story.

m) Monitor time and content of **television** and movie viewings.

n) Encourage your child to take **responsibility** (e.g. helping to set the table and picking up toys).

o) With any of your **child's fears**, reassure her that you will make sure that nothing bad will happen to her.

p) **Provide** your child with **opportunities** to sort, group, match, count and sequence with real-life situations (e.g. setting a table).

q) Help your child understand and cope with strong feelings by giving her words to use when she is angry (e.g. "I can see that you are sad about going home" or "angry at your friend").

r) Play games with your child that teaches **left and right directions**.

s) Enhance your five-year-olds experience with **trips** to the park, library, zoo, etc.

t) Always show **affection**.

u) **Avoid physical punishment**, since it only promotes fear, guilt and teaches your child that violence is acceptable in certain situations. Instead, send the child to a quiet, boring place without anything to do for a few minutes.

5. DEVELOPMENTAL SCREENING AND RED FLAGS

It is important to review and repeat developmental screenings at every age of your child's life in order to assess progression, regression, or any difficulties. Developmental skills are to be mastered by the appropriate age in 85-90% of children. Although each child is unique, some children have not yet mastered a skill due to various contributing factors such as developmental problems, lack of opportunity to learn or practice, cultural norms, parent/child interaction, environmental limitations or prematurity (i.e. premature infants may develop later than their peers). Review the following developmental screening to assess your child's development. If you check one or more "no" responses or a *red flag* is present, then discuss with your child's health professional.

PHYSICAL DEVELOPMENT

Gross Motor Skills:
- Hops on one foot without support
- Walks up the stairs with alternating feet
- Starts, stops, and changed directions when running
- Throws and catches a bouncing ball most of the time
- Climbs playground equipment without difficulty

Fine Motor Skills:
- Draws a stick person with at least 3 body parts
- Draws lines, simple shapes and a few letters
- Able to copy a cross symbol
- Cuts and pastes using symbols
- Holds a pencil correctly (between thumb and forefinger)

YES	NO

SOCIO-EMOTIONAL DEVELOPMENT

- Plays well in a group (shows interest in playing with others)
- Follows the direction of a group
- Shares willingly with others
- Separates easily from you
- Engages in a variety of activities
- Expresses a wide range of emotions
- Shows concerns and care towards others
- Understands the feelings of others
- Follows simple rules

YES	NO

SPEECH AND LANGUAGE DEVELOPMENT

Receptive Skills:
- Identifies the sounds at the beginning of some words (e.g. "papa" starts with the "puh" sound)
- Responds verbally to simple questions such as "hi, how are you?"
- Understands questions and senses (e.g. what do you do with your ear?)
- Able to explain the function of objects with better reasoning

Expressive Skills:
- Speaks clearly most of the time
- Uses almost all sounds of the language with few or no errors
- Correctly states simple words such as zoo, horse, buzz, much, chop, jam, fridge, shoe, look, push, etc
- Some lisp and may have difficulty with sound of "l, r, s, k, sh, ch, etc)

	YES	NO

COGNITIVE DEVELOPMENT

- Understands directions involving "if..then"
- Understands the placing of objects "on, under, in front of, behind"
- Describes past, present, and future events
- Knows all the letters of the alphabet
- Prints the first letter or more of her name
- Counts to 10
- Knows the common primary colours and shapes
- Tells stories and uses sentences to describe objects and events
- Understand 2-part commands

	YES	NO

SELF-HELP AND ADAPTIVE SKILLS

	YES	NO

- Dresses and undresses with little help
- Pours drinks (e.g. milk, juice) without spilling
- Able to feed himself (e.g. uses spoon, fork, etc)
- May perform self-care tasks (e.g. brushing teeth, hand washing)
- Works independently sometimes
- Tolerates frustrations and failures
- Able to draw the self
- Cares for own toilet needs
- Responds appropriately to potentially harmful objects

For the following "Definite Red Flags", consult your child health professional, if one or more of your answers is "yes".

DEFINITE RED FLAGS

	YES	NO

- Loss of any previously obtained skills
- Does not respond when name is called
- Rarely engages in social interaction or seems aloof with other kids and adults
- Preoccupation with unusual interests (switches, doors, etc)
- Performs activities in special or certain sequences
- Prone to temper tantrums (especially when rituals are interrupted)

Please note that developmental screening checklists are not 100% or case sensitive. As such, always consult with your child's health professional regarding any developmental concerns.

SECTION 2:
Important Motor Developmental Milestone Stages

HEAD CONTROL

GENERAL

Babies are born with little ability to control their head and neck muscles. They are born with a relatively large head that is heavy for their bodies and with limp neck and back muscles (since they are curled up in the womb).

The ability to develop good head control depends on the head and neck muscles reinforcement, which occurs in increments within the first six months of life. Your baby's ability to lift his head indicates the beginning of motor development and body control. It is difficult for young babies to hold their heads and thus they require support. It takes a great deal of effort for them to lift their head against gravity. However, once this ability is mastered, your baby will be able to hold his head still, lift it, turn it to the side, etc.

Babies try to lift their heads because of the natural instinct to develop and control the body and the innate curiosity to discover their surroundings. Other than the obvious reasons for developing the body and muscles surrounding the area of the head and neck (one of the most important parts of the body), head control is also necessary for swallowing solid foods and sitting in a high chair.

TIP: Because the muscles of the newborn and young infant are weak, and he does not control the movements, his head should be supported with caution when he is moved. Besides muscle weakness of the neck, initially the baby has relatively a larger head-heavy to support.

STAGES OF DEVELOPMENT: HEAD LIFTING

Month 1	- By the end of the first month of life, he will manage to lift his head briefly and turn it from side to side while lying on the stomach.
Month 1 – 2	- Your baby is gaining some control of his head and is able to lift it off the floor while leaning on the forearms and moving his head from side to side. - If he is especially strong, he will raise his head while lying on his back. - When you carry your baby on the shoulder, he will have enough control to hold his head up shortly but not for long.
Months 2 – 3	- Not yet strong enough to support the head.

Months 3 – 4	- Able to raise head to a 45-degree angle while lying on his stomach and keeps it steady. - He should also be able to hold his head in line with the rest of the body as it is pulled up. - There is significant improvement in head control at this age.
Months 4 – 5	- The baby can lift his head and chest while leaning on his elbows and can lift off the floor when leaning on his hands with his chest.
Months 5 – 6	- By six months of age, he will be able to hold his head steadily and erect, and be able to flex it forward when he is pulled into a sitting position.
Months 6 – 7	- By this age, most babies are able to sit up alone for short periods.

CHECKING BABY'S HEAD & TRUNK CONTROL

To check your baby's head control, you may do the following:
- Sit the baby on your lap or on a firm object.
- Provide just enough shoulder or trunk support to keep the child sitting upright.
- Gently lessen the head support you are providing him to see if he can hold or partly hold his head up, even if it is just for a moment.
- Catch your child's head softly with your fingertips when it begins to fall.

COMMENT: To check the baby's head tone, the doctor will hold your baby in the air to see that he holds his head in line with his body as he is pushed into a sitting position.

To check your baby's trunk control, you may do the following:
- Sit your baby firmly and hold his body just under his arms.
- Gradually move your hands lower on his body to find out how low the support can be for him to keep him in an upright position.
- If your baby can keep his balance and remain sitting upright when you hold him low at the hips, then he is developing fairly good trunk control.

CAUSES OF DELAYED SITTING, HEAD AND TRUNK CONTROL

Possible causes of delayed sitting, head and trunk control can be (a) central neurological or brain disorders such as cerebral palsy and brain malformations; (b) neuromuscular conditions such as spinal muscular atrophy; or (c) global developmental delay, which can initially present with delays in gross motor skills.

> **TIP: Sleeping on the Back & Development of Head Control**
> - Infants sleep on the back to prevent SIDS (Sudden Infant Death Syndrome). This is associated with slightly slower gains in head control. This disadvantage can be easily overcome if the infant has supervised playtime on the stomach.
> - Side & back sleepers are less likely than stomach sleepers to be able to raise their head at a 45-degree angle and lower it with control at 56 weeks of age.

ENCOURAGING HEAD LIFTING

To encourage your baby to lift his head, you may try to do the following:
- Lay your baby on his stomach on a soft blanket several times throughout the day. The blanket should not be too soft so that he will not be "drawn in it". Gradually increase the time that your baby lies on his stomach to develop and strengthen the neck muscles.
- From two months of age, place bright and eye catching colors and toys in front of the baby. Lie opposite to your baby and talk to him.
- Lay your baby on your stomach face to face and talk to him.
- Place a rolled-up towel under his chest and help him place his hands on the floor.
- From three to six months of age, you may want to prop your child up in a chair or on the bed with lots of head and neck support (pillows are good). You may also place your baby on his back and slowly pull him up by his hands to a sitting position. Slowly ease his back down and repeat.

COMMENTS: SWINGS, BOUNCERS, and JUMPERS & HEAD CONTROL

SWINGS
- The swing is designed to rock a small infant or child.
- A swing will never substitute for human contact, so you should use it sparingly.
- However, swings may help soothe the fussy baby and provide exhausted parents with a few moments of quiet time.
- Check to ensure that the swing is safe for your baby when your baby is less than six months of age.
- Stop using the swing when the baby reaches 15-20 months.
- Do not use the swing as a substitute for supervision.
- Limit the amount of time your baby spends in the swing, as he can get dizzy.

BOUNCERS

- A young baby's neck is not strong enough yet to support his head when he is jiggled and jostled a lot. Though securing your baby in a baby carrier or a sling while you jog may seem like an ideal way of getting your exercise and keeping your baby happy, the bouncing could be risky. Instead, strap him in a stroller when you go for a jog.
- Bouncer seats or baby rockers can be intolerable for parents of young infants. They may help calm the fussy baby and give parents a break, but allow your baby to be near you for safety reasons.
- Some bouncers can bounce or rock back and forth, using your baby's weight and heights. Ensure that they are safe before placing your baby in one.

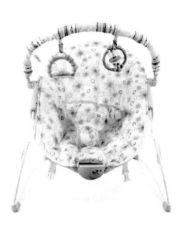

JUMPERS

- Some experts state that the use of jumpers can cause certain kinds of injuries to bones and joints, so be careful and time-wise when using jumpers.

Parent's Role – Holding Your Baby's Head

a) Since baby's neck muscles are weak at birth, you need to support his head and neck for at least the first few months of life or so. You will need to cradle your baby's head and neck in the palm of your hand when you take him out of the crib or carry him from one place to the other.
b) Stimulate to let the head turn.
c) Place him on tummy and put colored toys in front of him to stimulate attention and get him to lift head (after one month of age).

WHEN TO BE CONCERNED AND CASE DESCRIPTION

When your baby seems to be struggling to lift his head up even slightly by three months of age, discuss with your child's health professional. Remember that premature babies reach later developmental milestones.

> **Case Description:** my six-month old baby lacks head control. When he looks at something, his movement is jerky and he cannot hold his head up well. My baby does not make much of an attempt to stand and push on his legs when you hold him and his spends a lot of time in the car seat.
> Remember that markers of development are average, so not every child will be comfortable as quickly as others. Your baby may be well advanced in his development in one area and may not be in others, which is normal. However, one would expect a child at six months to achieve greater control over positioning the neck and head muscles, so consult your doctor for a developmental assessment.

ROLLING OVER

GENERAL

Rolling over is one of your baby's first steps in being able to move from one place to another and a key step towards sitting and walking. It is an important stage in motor development and proves that your baby is developing muscle mass. These muscles are crucial in helping the baby learn how to sit, crawl and perform other activities. While babies often flip from the front to the back first, doing it the other way around is perfectly normal too. Some babies never roll over; they skip it entirely or simply move on to sitting or crawling. Some may even adopt it as their primary mode of transportation.

WHEN TO EXPECT

Some babies can flip themselves from front to back as early as **3 months of age**, however most babies require strong neck and arm muscles especially to flip from back to front (which usually develop around **5-6 months of age**). Rolling over usually begins with rolling front to back before being able to roll from back to front (rolling from front to back is easier than the other way). The following are factors that affect when your baby will begin rolling:

- **Maturity** (e.g. a premature baby may be delayed in rolling over)
- **Personality** (a baby with a mellow personality tends to be slightly slower in motor development than his more active counterparts)
- **Body size** (larger and bigger babies start rolling over on average later than leaner or smaller babies; a plump, placid baby may be later in beginning to roll over)
- **Sleeping on the back** (leads to a slight delay in rolling over)

HOW IT DEVELOPS

AGE	HOW IT DEVELOPS
About 3 Months of Age	▪ When the baby is placed on her stomach, she will lift her head and shoulder high, using the arm for support. ▪ These mini push-ups help strengthen the muscle and will be used to help in rolling over. ▪ At this point, she may be amazed (or amaze you) that she is able to flip from back to front and vice versa.
At 5 Months of Age	▪ Your baby will lift her head up, arms up and arch her back while pushing her legs and "swimming" with the hands. This helps muscle development.
By 6 Months of Age	▪ Learns to roll over in both directions, front to back and back to front.

THE PARENT ROLE

- Parents can help stimulate the rolling movement process of their babies. It is important that parents make the process an enjoyable one and not an uncomfortable experience. Some babies arch their heads back, and then flip over to their back, but this is not always true or considered controlled rolling. Actual rolling involves tucking one arm and shoulder under, then pushing off with the other arm and legs.
- Since much of the early difficulties with rolling involve getting the arms and legs into the proper position (one arm and shoulder tucked under the body and the other arm and leg pushing), parents can help guide their baby through the motion to stimulate a roll.
- A great way to encourage rolling over in your baby is by providing her with tummy time each day (trying for a certain period of time each day). Offer different objects to get your baby interested in rolling over such as a big ball to the side of her or toy or book, etc. If you notice your child rolling on her own, wiggle a toy to the side of her to see if she rolls to it. If your baby does not roll over, then try again at another time.
- Applaud your child's efforts and smile for the reassurance and security your baby needs.

> **SAFETY TIP:** Remember to never leave your baby unattended on an elevated surface since babies generally start to roll over around 3 months of age. Some babies can roll back from the stomach, and almost panic since they do not know how to get back onto their backs. Comfort your baby and show her the motion slowly of how to turn over.

WHEN TO BE CONCERNED

CONSULT YOUR CHILD'S DOCTOR IF:
- Your baby does not figure out how to flip one way or the other by 6-7 months of age and is not showing any interest in getting around by any other means.
- Your child has not moved onto sitting or even trying to move around

PARENT CONCERN:
I put my 5-month old baby to sleep on her back but during the night she flips over onto her stomach. Should I worry about SIDS (Sudden Infant Death Syndrome)? Should I check her frequently during the night and flip her back to her back?

ANSWER:
According to the AAP (American Academy of Pediatrics), when infants are able to easily turn over from their backs to their stomachs, they should still sleep on their backs in whatever position they prefer. Although infant's risk of SIDS could be increased slightly, if the infant spontaneously flips onto her stomach, the risk is not sufficient to outweigh the great disruption to the parents. Parents do not need to keep checking on their babies after he/she is let down to sleep. By about 6 months of age, most infants have the ability to turn over, and those who prefer to sleep on their stomach usually do. It is impossible for parents to stop their infants from turning over once they have the ability to do so. There is still a risk of SIDS for older infants, but the risk is very low. Even though you have lost control over your infants sleeping position, you always have control over the environment he/she is in. As well, it is important that the sleep environment is safe.

SITTING

GENERAL

Sitting offers your baby a new view of the world. Similar to many other milestones, sitting is a skill that develops in stages. Typically, babies sit with no support (securely and holding objects in their hands) around **six to eight months of age**; some even sit as early as four months and others, as late as nine months.

Once your baby is able to sit, it is only a matter of time before your baby begins crawling. It is certainly an important milestone prior to starting solids. The ability to sit unsupported (around 6-7 months of age) and to pivot while sitting (around 9-10 months of age) provides increasing opportunities to manipulate several objects at a time and to experience a novel combination of objects.

WHEN IT DEVELOPS

The ability to sit begins with the ability to control one's own head, which is a skill your baby is building as she sits without support on your lap.
Around the age of four months, the baby's head and neck muscles strengthen rapidly. Your baby will learn to raise and hold her head up while she is lying on her stomach. Then, she will figure out how to prop herself up on her arm and hold her chest off the ground (similar to a mini push-up).
By the age of four months, she may be able to sit **momentarily without assistance**. However, you still need to stay close by to provide support, including the use of a pillow to cushion a possible fall. Initially, she will be **leaning** forward on one or both arms. She will then figure out how to maintain her balance while seated.
Around the **age of seven months**, the baby will probably be able to **sit unsupported** and gradually learn how to turn when sitting to reach a desired object. At this point, she will try to get into a sitting position when lying on the stomach, by pushing up on her arms.
By the **age of eight months** (ranges from 5-9 months), most babies will be **sitting well without support** independently. At this age, most have the trunk and pelvic strength to maintain unsupported sitting.
Also, once your baby is able to figure out that she can lunge from a sitting position and balance on her hands and knees, she will be almost ready to crawl (see *Crawling*).

> **CLUE: Readiness to Sit**
> When your child is not strong enough or at an early age and placed in a sitting position, she will prop forward and gradually, she will be able to sit with a straight back (once the neck and back muscles strengthen). Note that your child's back gradually straightens in the first few months of life. Around 6-9 months of age, your baby will learn to sit up unaided. At first, the baby may tilt sideways or backwards, so you may want to surround her with cushions to soften any falls. A clue that your child is ready to try sitting is when she is able to push up on her chest while lying on her belly.

SOME CAUSES OF LATE SITTING

These include familial problems, mental abnormalities, muscle or hypo/hyper-tonia (e.g. cerebral palsy, delayed maturation and environmental factors such as emotional deprivation).

THE PARENT ROLE

- Sitting with support – give your baby an opportunity to sit with support from the age of 2 months. Use good support to his neck and back. Watch your baby at all times.
- **Encourage your baby to play when face down** on the floor. Then, prompt your baby to look up, lifting her head and chest to see toys or your face. This helps strengthen your baby's neck and back muscles (necessary for achieving the sitting position).
- Before your baby is able to sit well, **practice the sitting position** with her when she is well rested. Learning to sit requires plenty of practice on the baby's part and great assistance from the parents and/or caregivers.

- Once your child is able to sit, **place a toy in front** of her (one that you can dangle) and watch as she tries to reach for it, one hand at a time. You can also **move a toy** from one side to the other. This will make your child move her arms and reach for it while sitting.
- You can have **tummy time** and have your baby do mini push-ups when you lay your baby across your legs and make lift up or push up off the floor with her hands. Supervised tummy time is very important for the development of head control, arm and trunk strength.
- Get down on the floor with your baby and play with her, allowing her to practice sitting with your support until she is eventually sitting without your support.
- **Avoid slowing the developmental process**: While there may not be much a parent can do to speed up the process of when your child begins to get into the sitting position, there are ways to avoid slowing the developmental process such as the following:

  - *A baby who is propped up at an early age (in an infant seat, stroller, etc) or receives a lot of practice at this early age being in a sitting position may slow the process of sitting on her own and unsupported.*
  - *A baby who spends the majority of her time lying on her back (e.g. baby carriers) and is rarely propped up to sit may begin sitting at a later age as well.*
  - *An overweight baby is another factor that may slow the sitting process down.*

WARNING SIGNS

Warning Sign: Consult your child's doctor if you answer no to the following since this indicates a warning developmental sign.

- ❐ Does your child support or hold her head by six months of age?
- ❐ Is your child able to prop herself up on her arms?

CRAWLING

GENERAL

The crawling stage is one of the most fun, most exciting & overwhelming experiences of your child's development. However, it can become exhausting, as you constantly need to have an eye on your baby's every move. Crawling helps strengthen your baby's muscles for vital motor skills and boosts physical abilities (which will help for the walking stage). It also improves fine motor skills (while holding an object, examining it and dropping it) and visual motor skills (develops perspective and 3-D world).

WHEN TO EXPECT

Generally, most babies crawl between 6 and 10 months of age. For some babies, crawling at an early age can mean that they begin lying on their stomach earlier (in which they will need plenty of supervised playtimes). If crawling occurs later, less time may be spent on the stomach. It is also normal for some babies to not crawl at all and go directly to the pull-to-standing and walking stage (when they have not been given the chance to develop crawling abilities).

These babies will not learn how to raise their bodies or place their hands and knees in any sort of locomotive action. In some scenarios, there are babies who will opt for bottom shuffling instead of crawling where they gather on their stomachs or move directly to pulling up, standing, or walking.

HOW IT DEVELOPS

Crawling typically occurs after the baby is able to sit well without support (around 6-7 months of age). As your baby's muscles strengthen (arms, legs and back), he will be able to go from the sitting position to the crawling position. Over time, he will be able to master the advanced positions of **cross crawling** -moving one arm and the opposite leg together when moving forward, rather than using an arm and a leg from the same side. When he reaches about 9 months and gains more experience, he will be able to go from a crawling position back into a sitting position!

CRAWLING STYLES

Most babies will find a way of moving around, either by crawling on their hands and knees or wiggling forward on their bottoms. Each baby is unique and moves around in distinctive ways. The following are the 3 most common types of crawling:

BELLY CRAWL
Creeping or moving about on the stomach (wiggling forward on stomach).

CLASSIC CRAWL
Travelling on hands and feet (a stage many reach just before walking).

CRAB CRAWL
Crawling backwards or sideways (not getting the hang of going forward for a while) See note.

BOTTOM SHUFFLING: Bottom shuffling is an uncommon variant of crawling. It can cause delay in acquiring independent walking. The infant, who bottom shuffles, typically does not crawl, dislikes the prone position, and reluctant to stand and/or walk. When held under the arms, he might adopt the "sitting on air position". Although bottom shuffling is a normal variant, it can be associated with abnormal causes (e.g. cerebral palsy).

THE PARENT ROLE

Stay calm, relax, and be patient while encouraging your baby to begin crawling. Given enough time, crawling may just happen instinctively. Helpful tips of how to encourage crawling for a few minutes each day:

- ✓ **Spend time on the floor with your baby** while he is lying on his stomach (preferably on carpeted flooring). Face him on the floor directly so that he can look at your face while you talk, amuse, and encourage him to go look for a toy.
- ✓ Attempt to get some measure of the distance between the floor and his upper body in the supported position allows him to lift his head. Get a roller with approximately the same measurements. Place the roller underneath his upper body with arms hanging over the front of the roller. This supported position allows him to lift their head and discover his surroundings.
- ✓ You may also place a dog-borne pillow on a rolled towel under his chest when he is on his stomach to keep his head up so that he may look around and enjoy what he sees.
- ✓ Place something hard behind his feet to give him something to push up against when trying to crawl.
- ✓ Gently hold elbows and draw both elbows towards the baby's body to help him lie on his elbows; be sure to continue providing support.
- ✓ **Cover your baby's knees** since bare knees on a cold surface, hard floor or itchy carpet can be uncomfortable and may even discourage crawling.
- ✓ Never leave your baby **unattended**.
- ✓ Use colored toys that roll. It will encourage the baby to crawl but also enhance coordination between hands and eyes when he tries to reach for the toy.
- ✓ Use a toy he likes and put it on the side of your leg so he will try to go over your leg and get the toy.

> **TIP: Childproofing Your Home** - Before your baby starts crawling, childproof your home:
> - Keep hot foods away from the edges of tables and countertops to prevent any burns.
> - Keep toiletry out of the baby's reach.
> - Use door straps to protect your baby's fingers.
> - Place safety plug outlets covers and hide electrical cords behind furniture.
> - Cover or block access to radiators and floor heaters.
> - Attach corner and edge guards to secure furniture.
> - Poison proof your home.

WHAT'S NEXT?

Once your baby masters crawling, then he will attempt steps to learn how to walk. Around 9-10 months of age, your baby will learn that pushing off with the knees gives him the boost required to become mobile. He will begin pulling up on everything that is within reach! Once he has a feel for balancing his legs, he will be ready to stand on his own and cruise while holding onto things. It is only a matter of time until he begins walking, running, and jumping!

PREDISPOSING FACTORS FOR DELAYED CRAWLING

- Most days are spent in a crib, stroller, baby carriers, etc.
- Mostly lying on their backs
- Not enough time spent on the floor
- Infant walkers used (eliminates desire to learn to crawl)
- Toys brought to the baby, etc.

WHEN TO BE CONCERNED

Babies develop skills at their own unique pace. As long as other milestones are reached, this may not be a concern. Consult your child's health professional if your baby has…

- Shown no interest in becoming mobile by any means (whether it is creeping, crawling, rolling, or scooting)
- Cannot move his arms or legs together
- Does not learn to use both arms and legs equally
- When physical development and motor skills seem to be generally slow or not progressing normally.

Remember that rolling over, sitting without support, cruising & walking independently are important developmental milestones – crawling is not.

PARENT CONCERN: Should I get my crawling baby shoes?

Most parents are eager to shoe shop for the young child who is about ready to start walking. Do not invest in shoes just yet; wait until your child masters walking and has a feel for balance.

STANDING

GENERAL

- Standing is a major milestone in your child's life, typically reached around 9-10 months of age.
- Standing is considered one of the most important gross motor (large muscle) milestones, because it shows that your infant has stability and strength in his legs and trunk to support his body. Stability and strength are necessary requirements for the next big accomplishment of cruising (walking while holding on) and finally, walking.
- Keep in mind that even though infants are able to stand with support, they usually cannot pull themselves up to a standing position on their own until they are 8-10 months of age. A baby who stands erect and unsupported for about ten seconds or more is standing alone.
- It is important to remember that infants often surprise you! You never know when your baby may decide to try pulling himself up to stand. As such, play it safe and lower the crib mattress as soon as your baby turns 6 months old.

WHEN WILL MY BABY STAND?

Usually, infants will:
- ✓ Stand, holding on to objects between 6 ½ months to 8 ½ months of age
- ✓ Pull up to a standing position between 8 to 10 months of age
- ✓ Stand for about 2 seconds between 9 to 11 ½ months of age
- ✓ Stand alone between 11 to 13 ½ months of age

Around the age of **ten months**, your baby will probably be able to use his legs to support his own weight; however, he will still need you to help maintain his balance. Around **10-11 months** of age, your baby will be happy to discover that he can pull himself up to a standing position with or without your help. When your baby does pull himself up for the first time, he will certainly be excited and very happy with himself.

IS MY BABY READY TO STAND

- Around the age of 8 months is when your baby should be ready to stand.
- If your baby is actively getting up on his feet and enjoying himself, it is a positive sign that his legs are physically strong enough to bear his own weight.
- At 8 months of age, parents can explore upright positions at an earlier age without any risks of detrimental effects such as bow legs or spinal problems.
- Regardless of starting your baby upright early, you will find that all babies have legs that look slightly bowed; it will straighten as your baby grows.

PREPARING MY BABY TO STAND

- To help prepare your baby to stand, you should help him strengthen his legs since standing requires strong leg muscle development.
- In order to help strengthen your baby's muscles, you can hold your baby's hands while he is sitting down. Slowly raise his arms above his head to help lift him up into a standing position. Allow your baby to stay in this position for a few seconds and then slowly place your baby back in a sitting position. Repeat this procedure several times a day to help strengthen your baby's hands, arms and legs.
- Bouncing your baby on your lap encourages him to bounce up and down, strengthening his muscles.
- Expose your baby to play time on the floor and as much of it as he wants to help him stand at an earlier age.
- The use of bouncers and walkers that promote earlier standing and walking are not needed to help strengthen your baby's muscles.

Playing It Safe

- Lower your baby's crib mattress to prevent her from falling over, since the crib is one of the first places your baby will learn to stand.
- Supervise your baby as he tries to stand since he will often fall right back down into a sitting position; however, allow your baby to try and getting back up on his own using safe furniture in the surroundings (e.g. chair, sofa, etc).
- Keep hazardous or dangerous pieces away from your baby's reach including a vase, clock, bowls, etc. Remember that your baby will grasp at anything within reach to help him stand up.
- Ensure that there are no sharp edges on the objects your baby uses for support and make sure that each piece of furniture is sturdy enough to hold your baby's weight.

Preparing Your Baby to Return to a Sitting Position Safely

- When your baby is an upright position, try to bend his knees a little when holding onto him.
- Guide your baby slowly into a sitting position and loosen your hold a bit as he is a few inches away from the floor.
- Repeat this safely several times throughout the day and eventually, your baby will be able to get himself into a sitting position safely.

WALKING

GENERAL

Walking is one of the most important milestones in your child's life. The American Academy of Pediatrics (AAP) considers the developmental window for walking to range between 9-18 months of age. The age at which a child first steps out is not a reflection of intelligence or future success in various areas (e.g. athletic). Those who walk early may have athletic difficulties later on. Many athletic children walk in time or later. Early walkers are not smarter than late walkers.

Once your child starts walking, you may notice some structural and walking irregularities or difficulties. Toddlers have a different structure in their feet compared to adults, often leading parents to believe that there is a problem. Generally, this is not the case and the majority of children do not have any foot or gait problems. Most differences are developmental and will change as the child grows.

WHEN IT DEVELOPS

The majority of children do not start walking until after the first birthday. Though the average child begins walking around the age of 13 months, there is a wide disparity for when children reach this milestone. Some babies begin walking as early as 8 months, while others take much longer. Most take their first steps between 9-12 months of age and are walking well by the time they are 14-15 months. However, many perfectly normal children do not begin walking until they are 16-17 months. Some babies cruise for months before getting up the nerve to let go and walk on their own.

FACTORS INFLUENCING THE DEVELOPMENT OF WALKING
- **Genetic Makeup**: Early or late walking runs in families.
- **Siblings**: Older siblings may speed things up since the young baby may try to keep up with brothers or sisters; siblings can be an important motivator.
- **Weight/Build**: A muscular baby is more likely to walk earlier than a plump child. A child with short and sturdy legs may walk earlier than a child with long and slender legs that are more difficult to balance.
- **Personality:** A child who is a risk-taker is more likely to get the nerve to try walking sooner than a naturally cautious child.
- **Crawling:** A child who is an ineffective crawler or who does not crawl at all may walk earlier than a baby who is happy crawling (some infants skip crawling; this is normal).
- **Negative Experiences**: An example of a negative experience may be a bad fall the first time your baby tries to walk, potentially delaying first steps.

- **Pressure**: Over-eager parents may cause your baby to rebel since he is not allowed to begin on his own time.
- **Inter-current illnesses**: These may place your baby's steps on hold until there is improvement or until your baby feels better.
- **Practice**: A baby who is given few opportunities (e.g. strapped in strollers, confined to bed for long time, a baby who bottom shuffles, overprotective parents) -limits what child does and chance to walk.

HOW IT DEVELOPS

The First Few Weeks
Holding your baby upright under the arms with the legs touching against a hard surface, your baby's feet will appear to be in a ready-for-walking position (know as walking reflex. this reflex disappears after two months)

5 Months
He bounces up and down, if you let him balance his feet on your thighs.

8 Months
He pulls himself up to stand while holding onto furniture. Over the next few weeks, he will get better at pulling himself up to stand. While he begins moving, try to let go and allow him to stand without support. Once he is able to do this, he may begin taking steps or picking up toys from a standing position.

9-11 Months
May begin walking and learn how to bend his knees and sit after standing.
At this point, he has probably mastered standing solo, stooping and squatting. He may even be walking, while holding on to your hand. However, it may take a few more weeks before he takes his first steps alone.

13-14 Months
About 75% of babies are walking on their own at thirteen months, albeit unsteadily. If your child is still cruising a lot, it may simply means that it is going to take a little bit longer. Some children do not walk until 16 or 17 months. By 14 months, he should be able to stand-alone and can probably stoop down and up again (may even be walking or walking backwards).

15-18 Months
The average child at this stage is pretty good at walking and likes to push and pull toys. By 16 months, he is probably interested in going up and down stairs, but requires your help for a few months. By the age of 18 months, most are proficient walkers. Although your baby can go up the stairs, many still need help getting back down for a few more months.

26 Months
Steps are more even, with the smooth heel-to-toe motion that adults use.

HELPING THE CHILD WALK SOONER

Signals for readiness to start walking:
- The **eager or adventurous** child may pull to stand alongside a chair or couch, let go and perhaps, take a step before falling. He will repeat this exercise until he succeeds.
- The **tentative** child will stand holding on for several weeks before trying to let go.
- The child with **little interest** in walking may suddenly begin around 13-15 months of age.

How to encourage your child to take first steps:
- ✓ Stand or kneel in front of your child and hold both of his hands, walking him towards you. You can bring a truck or car toy for him to hold onto and push.
- ✓ **Place** a piece of chocolate or other type of food **out of reach and call** him to try and take it.
- ✓ Walk together - you can help him gain confidence by **holding** both of his **hands** as he practices this new skill. Later, you may only hold onto one hand and have him grasp one or two of your fingers.
- ✓ Give your baby plenty of **time and space** for practicing, pulling up, cruising, standing and stepping into a room that does not have scattered rings or slippery floor. Allow your child to enter a room that is safe for pulling-up on furniture.
- ✓ Children love to **push toys** since it allows them to move around. Pushing a toy can strengthen arms, legs and core muscles; offer your child toys that he can push around (e.g. baby stroller, grocery cart).
- ✓ If your child falls, offer a quick hug or a reassuring word and send him on his way again.

CAUSES OF DELAYED WALKING

a) **Familial:** There is delayed maturation of nerve/muscle implicated with walking with the father, mother or sibling behaving in the same way. In such a case, other aspects of development are normal yet child development needs close follow up.
b) **Mental Delay:** Some children who are mentally delayed may be late in learning to sit and walk (e.g. children with Down's syndrome).
c) **Neurological Diseases:** Examples include cerebral palsy or hypertonia. Delayed walking may be seen in these cases (particularly with the spastic and athetoid type of cerebral palsy). In severe cases, walking may be impossible.
d) **Neuromuscular Problems:** These are uncommon. Gross motor delay may be seen early on, or delayed walking may be the first signs of trouble. Examples include the Duchenne's type and Muscular Dystrophy, vitamin B12 deficiency or peripheral neuropathy.
e) **Spinal Problems:** Spinal cord malformation/injury and deformity of the lower limbs may all be implicated as possible causes for delayed walking.
f) **Metabolic and Orthopedic Problems:** Examples include Rickets due to vitamin D deficiency (may present with irritability, convulsions due to low calcium, bone abnormalities, bowing of the legs, swelling of the end of the long bones, etc).
g) **Emotional Deprivation & Lack of Opportunity:** Children brought up in institutions may be late in sitting and walking, partly because of a lack of practice. Examples of these include illness or if the child is kept on his back for long periods of time may delay sitting or walking.

TIP: Blind children & Walking
Independent walking is delayed in blind children with only 50% walking by 24 months.

WHEN TO BE CONCERNED

Most children start to walk just after the age of one (13-15 months). If your child cannot walk, but is able to sit, crawl, roll over, move with help of objects, and stand, and is progressing in development (e.g. 15 months compared to 18 months of age) and the delay is in reasonable range, then there is probably no cause for concern (i.e. other milestones are developing normally). Remember that each baby develops differently and it is important to view the progression of skills in your child (some children will fall outside of the expected normal range of walking and yet, still be fine in the end).

Times to be concerned is when your child (a) is lagging behind significantly and/or when he is not walking by 18 months of age; (b) is walking only on his tiptoes (see chapter; (c) any difference at any stage particularly progressive between the movement of one side of the body compared to the other, favoring of a leg or reduced movement on one side compared with the other; (d) stiff legs or limping.

TIP: Starting to Walk & Walking Like A Penguin?
Most children make these early strides on tiptoes with their feet turned outwards (initially wide-based) and unsteady at the beginning. Your child may seem to be waddling like a penguin at first: legs wide feet turned out and arms held out (raised to the side to aid balance). By 18 months of age, your child will find his balance and walk more normally. Babies may also walk on the inside of their feet when barefoot.

PARENT CONCERNS

Are there any problems with my child walking early?
- If your baby is one of those eager and adventurous children, then let him walk and let him lead!
- Early walking (assisted or not) cannot cause bowlegs or worsen normal/physiologic bowlegs.
- If your baby is ready developmentally, allow him to practice his ability since exercise will strengthen some of the muscles used when walking alone; it will not hurt his legs. Simultaneously, a baby who does not want to "walk" at this time should NOT be pushed into it.

Should I train my late walker to walk?
- While you can help and encourage your child, there is little you can do to speed up the process as it is related to coordination, brain maturation and muscular strength. This varies from child to child.
- Do not pressure your child's locomotion, as it may interfere with his natural desire to try.

Are baby walkers helpful?
- There is no evidence that baby walkers help. Some experts discourage their use, since it makes it too easy for babies to get around, eliminating the desire to walk.
- Baby walkers slow the process of walking down, by letting the child move about without having to develop the needed balance (or how and when balance fails them; falling and picking themselves back up, etc), muscle coordination and strength required for walking.
- Babies are deprived of the visual cues that will help them figure out how their bodies walk through space since they cannot see their feet with walkers. These are vital steps to becoming a solo walker.
- Moreover, the constant use of a walker may cause confusion, as walking solo requires different body movements.

- There is also the risk of injury (e.g. fracture from tipping over and falling down stairs which both can lead to serious injury; also, use of walkers allow the baby to get near potentially dangerous items such as oven, electrical cords, etc).
- Walkers are not recommended for use for numerous reasons and the American Academy of Pediatrics (AAP) and the Canadian Pediatric Society (CPS) recommendations is that baby walkers should not be used.

Types of Feet, Legs & Walking

1) Flat Feet: It is normal in toddlers since foot muscles are not yet fully developed. Once the full heel-to-toe walking begins (around the age of 3-4 years), there should be an emerging arch. If not, then you should consult with your child's health professional (especially if there is a history of flat feet in the family).

2) In-toeing / Out-toeing: Children can outgrow these developmental occurrences by late childhood (9-10 years). There is actually nothing to treat in these cases unless it is interfering with daily life activities. Both in-toeing and out-toeing can occur due to foot rotation, leg, thigh or hip. Occasionally, severe in-toeing may cause a child to stumble as they catch their toes on the other heel. If your child sits on her legs in a v-shape (calves under thighs, toes pointed inward) or in a w-shape (bum on the floor, legs bent at the knee to either side), then you should encourage her to sit cross-legged instead.

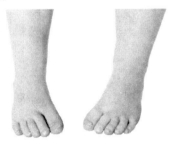

3) Bowed legs and knocked knees: Most babies are born with bowed legs, because of their folded position in the uterus. This normal developmental concern usually resolves itself by 2-3 years of age (as the child's bones straighten out). At that point, most children develop knocked-knee stance whereby the legs angle slightly inwards and typically lasting until the age of 6-7 years. However, bowed legs are not always normal and can sometimes be due to rare conditions such as Blount's Disease or Skeletal Dysplasia. Discuss these concerns with your child's health professional.

SECTION 3:

Recognition of Warning Signs and Symptoms of Developmental Disabilities

ADHD

Attention Deficit Hyperactivity Disorder

1. GENERAL
- ADHD is a chronic neuro-cognitive disorder, impairing and affecting different aspects of daily life. It is a medical, behavioural and developmental condition that relates to the brain's difficulties in organizing and processing information.
- **The incidence** of ADHD is 6-9% (up to 17%). In every classroom of 20 children, about 1-2 present with different degrees of ADHD. It is more common in boys than girls with a ratio of 3:1. However, boys behaviour is more noticeable, 7 boys to every 1 girl is referred for evaluation.
- Most children with ADHD (60-80%) will continue to present symptoms well into adulthood.
- The exact **cause** is not known with certainty; however genetics, anatomical and functional differences in various regions of the brain, environmental factors and toxins play a role.
- **The diagnosis** of ADHD relies on a number of symptom criteria.
- **Treatment** includes parent education, medication, family therapy, cognitive behavioural therapy, remedial intervention and skills training.
- **Accompanying disorders** may include learning disabilities, oppositional defiant disorder, conduct disorder, anxiety, mood disorder and depression.

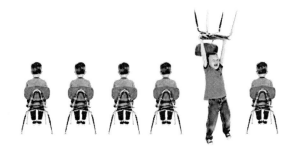

2. UNDERSTANDING THE SYMPTOMS AND PRESENTATION OF ADHD

General Symptoms & Criteria for Diagnosis
- Each child is unique and follows a unique timetable of development.
- Children develop at different rates and while a child may seem to be less mature than others, time itself may solve the problem .They can exhibit a large range of behavioural difficulties and are well known for short attention span, acting without thinking (often becoming overly excited) and full of energy. Often, these are the symptoms of ADHD .This is also the reason why it is hard to diagnose ADHD in toddlers.

- Some children develop the ability to sit, listen and follow age-appropriate commands by the time they enter preschool. Others achieve this by the time they enter kindergarten and nearly all children do so by the first grade.
- Children differ in activity levels as well as the capacity to be patient and the ability to focus, remember and organize themselves around certain tasks.
- For some children, **inattention, hyperactivity and/or impulsivity** remain past the 2nd or 3rd grade and may even intensify as the child grows. These children may suffer from ADHD and the symptoms may become more pronounced and easier to recognize with time.

- It is important to recognize the differences between a "discipline" problem and behaviours that are due to ADHD. For example, a child with ADHD may experience difficulties getting along with siblings, friends and classmates, whereas the "discipline" problem child may have one particular difficulty. Often times, teachers are usually the first to notice behavioural signs of possible ADHD.
- The diagnosis of ADHD may be difficult since it may be associated with other disorders (e.g. obsessive-compulsive disorder, learning disability). While many affected children experience learning difficulties, others do not and a diagnosis of ADHD may be delayed as a result.
- Because symptoms of ADHD are more obvious in some situations than in others and performance can vary depending on the particular situation, the diagnostic process can be more complicated for the clinician and for the family who do not, keep in mind its apparent and surprising variability. For examples, symptoms of ADHD are aggravated when the child faces a task which requires sustained attention or mental effort in a "non-interesting" activity (i.e. one that does not provide immediate pleasure) within a group setting (e.g. day care, school) or in a noisy, exciting situation.
- Symptoms are less intense in closely supervised situations, individual supervision or one-on-one conversations, as well as interesting activities with immediate benefits (e.g. video games).

What brings parents/caregiver to suspect the condition of ADHD?
- Parents and/or teachers become concerned when the child presents attention, concentration as well as learning difficulties and poor performance at school.
- **In day care**: Other suspicious features may include children who prefer free activities with action characters rather than learning close to a table, difficulty concentrating in a routine conversation, refusing to and not responding to instructions.
- **In school**: The child has difficulties listening in class (seems like his/her thoughts are elsewhere), difficulties following instructions, in studies, and organization, as well as not concentrating, disturbing others and a constant state of being "bored" (a common complaint of the ADHD child).

- Some parents will consult the health professional, because they themselves suspect ADHD and are concerned about their child's worrisome behaviours.
- Although signs of ADHD may be apparent in the preschool years, most families seek help when the child begins elementary school, particularly when the child's behaviour interferes with his adjustment and learning.
- Typically, boys are diagnosed earlier than girls. This is because boys with ADHD are more often agitated and exhibit more behaviour problems than affected girls who are more often " spacey "

3. Warning Signs for ADHD

Hyperactivity

- Individuals who are hyperactive have excessively high levels of activity, which may present as physical and/or verbal/emotional over-activity.
- Hyperactive children seem unable to control their reactions and will often blurt out inappropriate comments or act out without concern for others. This is known as emotional hyperactivity.
- It is often difficult to regulate activity levels of the hyperactive child, creating problems in school, social and work situations. Examples of symptoms of hyperactivity include:

Physical symptoms:
- Constant motion, perpetually "on the go" (as if driven by a motor)
- Difficulty keeping himself still
- Moves excessively (squirming, fidgeting, swinging feet)
- Often climbing and moving too fast
- Unable to stay in one place for long
- Is restless (getting up in the middle of homework or television)
- Tips over, breaks objects and runs into things
- Writes quickly or bad handwriting

Verbal symptoms:
- May talk excessively
- Talks so much that others do not have a chance to talk
- Interrupts others
- Monopolizes conversations

Emotional symptoms:
- Overwhelmed by waves of emotions
- Easily excitable
- Feels not "good enough"
- Low self-esteem
- Expects failures
- Blames himself
- Is forgetful and late
- Difficulty following instructions

Comment: Hyperactivity & Toddlers
Toddlers are usually in motion, rarely sit down, and resist being still, constantly jumping and moving from activities that require sitting for longer than a minute or two. Toddlers can be over-stimulated and over-excited. When there is a lot of stimulation, toddlers can become difficult to control (often crying or screaming). Young children may be disruptive (it is a display of their character).

Inattention

- **Paying attention** refers to the brain's ability (a complex neuro-cognitive process) to take all that is happening in the environment and immediately categorize and organize the information as relevant or irrelevant.
- When we pay attention, we:
  - Initiate (direct our attention to where it is needed or desired at the moment)
  - Sustain (pay attention for as long as needed)
  - Inhibit (avoid focusing on something that removes our attention from where it needs to be)
  - Shift (move our attention to our things as needed)
- Inattentive behaviours are sometimes overlooked, because they are harder to identify and less disruptive than hyperactive and impulsive symptoms.
- Although everyone experiences lapses in attention from time to time, the child with ADHD is faced with a chronic challenge in paying attention.
- Individuals who are inattentive have difficulty staying focused and attending to mundane tasks. **The child with ADHD simply cannot exercise control due to difficulties with:**
  - Sustaining attention long enough, especially to boring, tedious or repetitive tasks
  - Resisting distractions, especially to things that seem interesting or that fill in the gaps when sustained attention quits
  - Tune out of activities that are dull, uninteresting or un-stimulating
  - Not paying sufficient attention, especially to details and organization

- **Symptoms of inattention include the following**:
  - Easily distracted by irrelevant sights and sounds (e.g. alarms, music)
  - Careless mistakes due to distraction
  - Shifts from one activity to another or leaves unfinished homework for another activity
  - Requires constant guidance
  - Inability to listen (which may appear as disobedience)

- ❏ Difficulties following instructions
- ❏ Daydreaming or appears spacey
- ❏ Easily frustrated with homework
- ❏ Seems to get bored easily (i.e. the inability to sustain or follow through on tasks requiring prolonged mental effort)
- ❏ Trying to avoid activities that require a sustained effort or prolonged concentration
- ❏ Difficulties keeping up with items, frequently losing them and living life in a disorganized manner
- ❏ Difficulty keep track of belongings and forgetting routine items
- ❏ Difficulty organizing and completing tasks (specifically sorting out what information is relevant and irrelevant)
- ❏ Chronically disorganized with ideas, homework assignments, and time management

Comment: Inattention & Toddlers
Toddlers with ADHD are able to pay attention to certain interesting things, can focus on high-energy tasks and may have difficulty sustaining eye contact. Although attention may be below the norm at this age, it is not necessarily perceived as a problem.

Impulsivity
- Individuals who are **impulsive** have trouble inhibiting their behaviours and responses; they act on impulse rather than thought.
- **Symptoms of impulsivity include**:
  - ✓ Acting and speaking before thinking
  - ✓ Reacting in a rapid manner without considering consequences
  - ✓ May interrupt others, blurt out responses and rush through assignments without carefully reading or listening to instruction
  - ✓ Has no patience and cannot wait
  - ✓ Lack of impulse control (sometimes creates stress in school, work or relationships)
  - ✓ Does not take into account the danger or social impact of words and actions
  - ✓ May be seen as bossy, controlling or conflicting
  - ✓ May be rejected by peer groups due to impulsiveness
  - ✓ May appear withdrawn
  - ✓ Disrupts and interrupts others
  - ✓ Opts for speed over accuracy
  - ✓ Unable to keep powerful emotions in check, resulting in angry outbursts or temper tantrums

Comment: Impulsivity & Toddlers
The toddler with ADHD may jump off playground equipment, jump out of windows and run into the street, experience more accidents and falls, and break toys more frequently.

4. MYTHS ABOUT ADHD

Myth 1: All children with ADHD are hyperactive.
Fact: Some children with ADHD are hyperactive, but many others with attention problems are not. Children who are inattentive, but not overly active may appear to be spacey and unmotivated.

Myth 2: Children with ADHD can never pay attention!
Fact: Children with ADHD are often able to concentrate on activities they enjoy. However, no matter how hard they try, they have trouble maintaining focus when the task at hand is boring or repetitive. Lack of attention may be a symptom of a learning problem in which the child has trouble paying attention on one subject area, but not in others.

Myth 3: Punishing the child will control symptoms of ADHD.
Fact: Parents of children with concentration and attention problems tend to take responsibility and feel guilty about the child's situation. The fact that they cannot do much may lead to frustration, causing parents to punish the child. On the other hand, the child cannot behave as expected of him and fails to satisfy the parents. Everything he does may be followed with criticism and punishment. As such, he develops feelings of insecurity and being unloved.

5. DIAGNOSIS OF ADHD
- Since there is no single test that makes for the diagnosis of ADHD, criteria have been developed.
- The criteria for a diagnosis of ADHD are based on a classification system in the 4th edition of the Diagnostic and Statistical Manual of Mental Disorders (DSM-IV-TR), published by the American Psychiatric Association (APA).
- The following are the criteria for diagnosis:
    a) At least 6 out of 9 of the symptoms below of inattention and/or at least 6 of 9 symptoms below of hyperactivity/impulsivity must be present.
    b) Symptoms present early in life, before the age of 7.
    c) Symptoms are persistent for at least 6 months.
    d) Symptoms must be pervasive, occur in most settings (at home, school, social events, etc).
    e) Symptoms must be developmentally inappropriate for the child's age.
    f) Symptoms must be interfering with the child's functioning.

6. TYPES OF ADHD & SUB-TYPES

Combined Type = Classic Type (50-70% of cases)	<ul><li>Combination of hyperactive/impulsive and inattentive symptoms</li><li>Should include 6 or more symptoms of inattention above and 6 or more symptoms of hyperactivity/impulsivity for more than 6 months</li><li>Young child often has difficulties in the following:<ul><li>Starting and completing work (procrastination)</li><li>Ignoring relevant information and remembering what is really important</li><li>Keeping in mind only one thing at a time</li><li>Key areas of the school curriculum (e.g. immature behaviour in math like finger counting)</li><li>May be distractive, talking aloud, be in constant motion</li></ul></li></ul>
Predominantly Inattentive Type (25-35% of cases)	<ul><li>Displays 6 or more symptoms of inattention, but fewer than 6 symptoms of hyperactivity and impulsivity</li><li>Often loses things, forgets homework, daydreams, has trouble managing time, planning and organizing tasks</li><li>May appear selfish, lethargic and slow to respond or process</li><li>There are 2 subtypes within this type of ADHD:<ul><li>The first sub-type is children with major problems in concentration, organizational difficulties, and forgetfulness.</li><li>The second sub-type of the inattentive ADHD is children who often daydream and move slowly. This type is more common in girls than in boys.</li></ul></li></ul>
Predominantly Hyperactive / Impulsive	<ul><li>Displays 6 or more symptoms of hyperactivity/impulsivity, but fewer than 6 symptoms of inattention with symptoms persisting for more than 6 months</li><li>Least common type of ADHD</li><li>Characterized by restlessness and fidgeting, but with fewer problems in attention/concentration</li></ul>

AUTISM

Autism Spectrum Disorder

INTRODUCTION

- **Autism spectrum disorder (ASD)** is a developmental disability that causes substantial impairments in social interactions and communication along with the presence of unusual behaviours and interests. The **spectrum** refers to the continuum of developmental impairments that range from mild to severe.
- Autism typically begins before the age of 3 years and lasts throughout the lifetime. The mean age of parental suspicion is 14 months, though mostly seen by 24 months.
- The prevalence of autism is 1/150 with a ratio of 4:1 males. Its etiology is unknown.
- ASD is highly hereditary, evolving from a genetic susceptibility that involves multiple genes (though other factors have been discussed).
- For any developmental concerns, discuss with your child's health professional who will conduct screening tests to assess and refer for further developmental testing, if necessary. A complete comprehensive and diagnostic evaluation can be done by expert health professionals. Because appointments are usually difficult to obtain immediately, the diagnostic process can take some time; meanwhile, your child can be referred for early intervention.

TIP: Early Intervention
Early intervention is critical since it is the most effective way to speed up your child's development. It is conducted at home or at a childcare center. Early intervention will include a variety of behavioral, physical, speech and play therapy. Further treatment options include occupational therapy and special education services. The early establishment of appropriate management services in the early years of life can help minimize subsequent behaviour problems.

RECOGNITION: SIGNS & SYMPTOMS
General
- There is a wide range of signs and symptoms of ASD.
- The signs can be subtle and easily missed or they can be dramatic and overtly obvious.
- Although there are many presenting features associated with autism, most children do not show all of the features all the time. Instead, some children present with some features some of the time (all the signs do not have to be present for a diagnosis).
- An effective way to spot the problems at an earlier age is to keep a close eye on if and when your child is hitting the developmental milestones (e.g. social-emotional, cognitive). Note that while delays do not automatically signify autism, they do indicate a heightened risk for it or other problems.
- By 18-36 months of age, symptoms of autism are typically apparent. Subtle warning signs may be evident at a much earlier age, though speech and language problems are the most common presenting feature. Although most parents sense something is wrong with their child by 18 months, many do not voice these concerns until a later time when they realize that the child has little to no speech.
- In babies, ASD is a developmental disorder that presents differently at each developmental level. In addition, there is little research and clinical experience with ASD in babies. The DSM-IV-TR (the APA's manual for diagnosis) criteria are based on older children and are not relevant to infants (e.g. developing reciprocal friendships or developing intense interests in rituals).

Earlier Risk Markers in Babies: From 0-12 Months
The following are **risk markers** in babies from about 0 - 12 months or later: social smiling, eye contact impairment, temperament differences, visual tracking impairments, disengagement of visual attention and orienting to name.

You can ask yourself the following questions. For any concerns, consult with the health professional:
- Is your child unusually quiet and not demanding?
- Is he very irritable and difficult to console?
- Is there a 2-way social interaction/communication with gestures, words, babbling and/or frequent eye contact?
- Does your baby respond to warmth and is affective?
- Is he babbling in a non-typical way?
- Does he turn his head when his name is called (by 12 months)?
- Can he maintain joint attention?
- Does he greet people or wave bye?
- Is he demonstrating a few gestures?
- Does he look or point to objects when named?
- Does he extend his arms to be picked up and does not reach out in anticipation of being picked up?

Comment: Autism in Babies
Traits associated with autism such as poor social skills and reduce eye contact are likely to appear gradually as the infant reaches the end of the first year. Children do not exhibit characteristics of autism until at least 6 months of age. A new study shows that babies as young as one month of age may show atypical signs of autism, such as abnormal muscle tone and difference in visual processing. The signs are subtle and not something a parent would easily spot.

Early Diagnosis of Autism: Toddlers

The following are the **best discriminators** for an early diagnosis of autism in toddlers include:

- Joint attention (the most important and includes initiating and responding to joint attention)
- Eye contact
- Temperament
- Repetitive motor/sensory responses (many will not, but very concerning if it is the case)
- Attention to voice or response to name
- Abnormal play
- Hand leading

You can ask yourself the following questions and if there are any concerns, then discuss with your child's health professional.

- Does your child turn when his name is called?
- Can your child follow directions?
- Does he greet people or wave bye?
- Can he look or point to objects when named?
- Is your child able to point to named body parts?
- Does he enjoy listening to stories?
- Can your child answer questions?
- Did he stop talking or regress after saying a few words?
- Does he communicate using facial expressions, looking, reaching, showing, sounds, gestures, pointing and eye contact?
- Does your child echo phrases or sentences heard?
- Does he play with toys the way he is supposed to?
- Can he engage in group activities?
- Does he take an interest in playing with other children?
- Does your child initiate play with peers and/or siblings?
- Is your child crying or laughing for no apparent reason?
- Is he too interested by certain topics, toys and/or activities?
- Does he repeatedly line up toys?
- Does he ever pretend play?
- Has your child ever used his index finger to point to ask for something or indicate interest?
- How is your child's manner of play?

SYMPTOMS & SIGNS: EXPLANATIONS

Smiling & enthusiastic behaviour (by 4 months of age)
- By 4 months of age, your baby should typically respond when you make him laugh (e.g. tickling) and smile at him. He should be lighting up, overjoyed and happy.
- The child will make sounds to get the parents attention, smiles at sounds of familiar voices, play with others and imitate certain movements and facial expressions.
- The baby at risk does not smile back at you or smiles less often or less enthusiastically than expected (by 4 months of age). He is either late in smiling or does not smile at all.
- If the baby does not respond to you despite your attempts to interact and show affection, or if he seems self-absorbed and is not smiling back, then this is a cause for concern.

Temperament differences
- Sometimes, the earliest symptoms of autism are misinterpreted as a sign of a "good baby", because the baby is very quiet, passive and inactive (from birth).
- The infant at risk may be too content and happy to remain in his crib for long periods of time without babbling or crying for food and prefers to be alone. He may show little interest in games or rituals and fails to develop preferential attachment to his parents. In fact, the child may be so non-reactive that parents wonder if he is deaf since he does not make any demands and is unusually quiet.

> **Comment**: Babies who are passive and inactive at 6 months of age and then extremely irritable or joyless at 12 months of age are at a higher risk of developing autism.

- In contrary to the above, the baby at risk may also be excessively irritable, a poor sleeper, picky eater and content only when clinging to one person. Small changes in routine may lead the baby to react violently (e.g. new food introduction, new food textures or methods of feeding).
- Babies can also cry for long periods of time and can be very irritable; they do not seek comfort (being difficult to console).

Eye contact impairment
- Some infants do not even look at their mothers when being fed and will avoid people's gaze. This feature is less important than the unusual quality of the gaze.
- An **eye gaze** refers to when the child is looking at the face of others to check and see what they are looking at and to signal interest in interacting (it is a non-verbal behaviour).
- The infant at risk for autism may tend to gaze briefly and out of the corner of his eye.
- In addition, **attentional disengagement** is when the child is not focusing his visual attention (i.e. eyes) towards a specific object or person.

> **Comment:** The child should seek and maintain eye contact when he is making a request. It is therefore important to look for the presence of sustained eye contact that is used socially with a range of people. Young ASD children may have adequate eye contact with their parents but may not when greeting strangers.

Cuddling & Orienting to Name
- Parents may realize that the infant is not typical from birth, because he does not like to be held in their arms (does not even reach to be picked up) and cannot be comforted. Also, the child at risk for autism may not turn his head when his name is called.

Babbling
- Typically, babbling begins by 6-9 months of age. The infant begins to vocalize repeated consonant vowel combinations in a monotone voice like "ba-baa".
- As vocal development continues, babbling sounds take on the characteristic of adult speech, even though the child may not have specific meanings in mind.
- Many infants babble when they wake up or when the mother comes to say " good morning ".
- The child, who sees and hears the mother, will smile and stop babbling. If the mother goes away for a second or stops talking to the baby, he will resume babbling and stop again if the mother talks yet again.
- However, the child at risk will continue to vocalize or babble as if he is not aware of his mother's speech. There is less eye contact and the mother may feel that the infant does not recognize her voice or notice when she enters or leaves the room.
- The atypical infant makes few vocalizations or has atypical ones ; instead of cooing or babbling, the infant may hum or grunt for extended periods, squeals stereotypically or laughs inappropriately.

Deficits of Social interaction & reciprocity
- **Social interaction** is the use of verbal and non-verbal behaviour used to convey or exchange information, express emotions and engage in interactions with others.
- **Non-verbal behaviours** include the eye gaze (i.e. looking at others faces to see what they are looking at and to signal interest in interaction), gestures (i.e. head and hand movements used)
- In the first year of life, infants use non-verbal behaviours to regulate social interaction and may use their eyes, face and bodily gestures and hands altogether to interact with others. At the same time, they learn to read or understand the non-verbal cues of others.

- Before learning how to talk, children often take turns with non-verbal behaviours in back and forth interactions. **Social reciprocity** is the back and forth flows of social interaction. It refers to how the behaviour of one person influences and is influenced by the behaviour of another person and vice versa.
- Impairments are found in social reciprocity as autistic children do not take an active role in social games, preferring solitary activities (a type of detachment seen even in small babies). Social isolation can lead to temper tantrums, self-impulsive behaviours, echolalia and so forth.
- Basic social interaction is difficult for children with autism since they are usually uninterested in interacting with others. They generally do not interact with children their own age, often avoid direct eye contact and glancing sideways rather than directly.
- The autistic child is unable to communicate in a way that most children do. Instead, he may develop inappropriate ways to communicate such as through aggression, self-injurious behaviours or tantrums.
- While some ASD children show little interest in or even awareness of other children, many others are in fact very interested in others (though lack the skills to interact typically and fail to maintain friendships). The quality and style of the child's peer interactions should be assessed, even if the child appears to be friendly and is quite talkative.

Joint attention (9-16 months of age)
- **Shared attention** is an early social deficit and the most disturbing characteristic in very young children with autism. It is defined as a normal occurring behaviour, whereby the infant shows enjoyment in sharing an object or event with another person by looking back and forth between the two and connecting.
- Change in the attention system occurs between 9-12 months of age. This allows the child to disengage his attention from the object he is playing with, shifting it to you and looking again at the object. This 3-part gaze is called **joint attention**.

- Infants learning to seek joint attention may use gestures to draw others attention to objects (e.g. holding out and showing an object or pointing to it).
- In older children, joint attention is manifested in gestures and speech and it develops in graduated stages.
- For example, if a child is playing with a toy, you (parent) is sitting close to him and somebody else asks him, "where is mom?" The typical baby will shift from playing with the toy, look at his mom and then reengage with the toy (the 3-part gaze).

- The infant at risk for autism will not disengage. He often takes no notice of the shift in gaze to signal such things as giving, reaching, pointing, head shaking), and facial expression (i.e. facial movements used to communicate with others and express emotion without the use of words).
- In the first year of life, infants use non-verbal behaviours to regulate social interaction and may use their eyes, face and bodily gestures and hands altogether to interact with others. At the same time, they learn to read or understand the non-verbal cues of others.
- Before learning how to talk, children often take turns with non-verbal behaviours in back and forth interactions. **Social reciprocity** is the back and forth flows of social interaction. It refers to how the behaviour of one person influences and is influenced by the behaviour of another person and vice versa.
- Impairments are found in social reciprocity as autistic children do not take an active role in social games, preferring solitary activities (a type of detachment seen even in small babies). Social isolation can lead to temper tantrums, self-impulsive behaviours, echolalia and so forth.
- Basic social interaction is difficult for children with autism since they are usually uninterested in interacting with others. They generally do not interact with children their own age, often avoid direct eye contact and glancing sideways rather than directly.
- The autistic child is unable to communicate in a way that most children do. Instead, he may develop inappropriate ways to communicate such as through aggression, self-injurious behaviours or tantrums.
- While some ASD children show little interest in or even awareness of other children, many others are in fact very interested in others (though lack the skills to interact typically and fail to maintain friendships). The quality and style of the child's peer interactions should be assessed, even if the child appears to be friendly and is quite talkative.

Comment: Temper tantrums are usually more intense and more frequent in the autistic child than in the typically developing child. Tantrums are often due to a child seeking attention, feeling overwhelmed, frustrated or hypersensitive to the environment or the child may even be trying to escape from a difficult task (e.g. protesting against a change in routine or trying to regulate himself in a more predictable way).

Pointing
- Between 12-16 months of age, the child's pointing to objects or people can serve and represent communicative and social functions.
- Typically while pointing to the desired object, the child looks back and forth between the object and the caregiver to be reassured that the caregiver understands his needs and to ensure that the object has been observed and appreciated.
- Most children with autism do not master this skill at the age-expected time and its absence by 18-24 months of age is a strong indicator of autism. Some children may make no attempt to elicit help and may just cry, while others may lead the parent/caregiver by the hands to the desired object and simply wait and cry).

Pretend play
- Typically, pretend play evolves in a predictable manner.
- By 4 months of age, the child will grasp objects, manipulate objects and sensory motor play will begin.
- By 8-10 months of age, the child will use toys to bang and throw around.
- By 12-14 months of age, the child begins to be aware of the intended use of objects and the imitation skills evolve.
- Pretend play emerges with time and increases in complexity and imagination.
- By 16-18 months of age, we begin to see the start of simple pretend play (e.g. telephone toy, feeding dolls).
- By 18-20 months of age, complex pretend play begins (e.g. changing dolls clothing for sleep, may use banana instead of telephone toys to talk).
- With autistic children, a lack or delay in pretend play is a relatively reliable sign of autism where the child may prefer particular toys (e.g. rocks, sticks, string of beads), play with toys in unusual ways (e.g. instead of playing with a miniature truck normally, the autistic child may turn it upside down or spin the wheels repeatedly), play constructively (e.g. stacking blocks, putting puzzles together, playing computer games) and so forth.

Delayed & disordered speech / language

- The most common presenting signs in a child later diagnosed with autism are communication / language skill deficits. However, parents do not verbal such deficits and do not usually raise concerns until the child's 2nd birthday (making such concerns less helpful in reaching early diagnosis).
- Children with autism experience difficulties with verbal and non-verbal communication.
- The development of verbal expression is generally delayed or, in rare cases, non-existent.
- Children do not talk (lack of babbling/words) or use language to communicate while others may talk in unusual ways (e.g. idiosyncratic language).
- Besides delayed or absent speech, there can be **language regression or atypical language**. The autistic child may present with the following:
  - ✓ Does not usually say any single words by the age of 15 months
  - ✓ Does not usually say 2-word phrases by 24 months
  - ✓ No babbling, pointing or making gestures by 1 year of age
  - ✓ Tone of voice or pitch is abnormal
  - ✓ Echolalia (the repetition of words, phrases, intonation, or sounds of others speech)

Note on echolalia: Echolalia is often mistaken for advanced speech in the child. It is more pervasive and enduring, because the child can remember and repeat chunks of speech (e.g. repeating a movie script, stories from books). Echolalia is only normal when it is temporary and occurs when toddlers are rapidly gaining word vocabulary and they only repeat the last 1-2 words of a sentence just heard.

- In terms of **language comprehension**, the autistic child may display the following:
  - ✓ Does not start or continue a conversation
  - ✓ Does not seem to want to communicate often
  - ✓ Has difficulties expressing needs or desires using typical words or motions
  - ✓ Does not respond to his name being called, but does respond to other sounds (e.g. car horn, ringing telephone)
  - ✓ Does not understand simple questions, statements or directions
  - ✓ Confuses pronouns and refers to the self as "you" and others as "I"
- Subtle social cues such as facial expressions, tone of voice and gestures are often lost along with language milestones (usually between 15-24 months).

- **Regression** of any kind should be taken seriously. Children with autism may develop normal/typical language skills and then regress in language skills, usually occurring between 15-24 months (particularly between 18-24 months). Parents may realize and report that the child stops talking, gesturing (e.g. pointing, waving bye), and makes less eye contact. For example, a child who spoke a few words and used his communicational abilities may stop using language entirely.

Repetitive movements and motor mannerisms
- **Repetitive movements** may include the following:
  - ✓ Abnormal and repetitive movements of body posture carried out in the same way over time (appears later than 2 years of age)
  - ✓ Head banging, finger flicking or twisting, taps ears, scratches and rubs a lot, stares at lights or switches lights on and off
  - ✓ Can show a restricted obsession with repetitive activities and interests (e.g. strong interest in particular objects or parts of objects and the repetitive movements within these objects)
  - ✓ Inappropriate ways of using objects
  - ✓ Obsessive attachments to unusual objects

Other sensory problems
- The following are other sensory problems that you may notice in the child at risk for autism:
  - ✓ Either under or over-reacts to sensory stimuli
  - ✓ Sudden noises can be upsetting and the child may respond by covering his ears and making repetitive noises
  - ✓ Can be highly sensitive to touch and texture
  - ✓ Not at all sensitive to smells, sounds, lights, textures and touch
  - ✓ Unusual use of vision or gazes (e.g. looks at objects from unusual points)
  - ✓ Does not cry when in pain
  - ✓ Likes order, routine and rituals
  - ✓ Extremes of temperament (easily upset, irritable or always happy and understanding)

SPEECH AND LANGUAGE DELAY

GENERAL INTRODUCTION

- **Communication** is a complex system of sounds, words and organized structure.
- Most children become extremely communicative by the age of 3 years, while others learn more slowly and with more difficulties.
- Learning to speak is a huge milestone in a child's life, occurring gradually through various interactions the child has with individuals and the environment.

- **Speech** is defined as the sound that comes out of our mouths, while **language** is involved with meanings of these sounds and serves as a measure of intelligence. Speech is the verbal expression of language and includes articulation (the way words are formed).
- **The causes** or contributing factors to speech and language delay are : prematurity, Autism, Learning disability, Hearing loss, maturation delay (late talkers), Extreme environmental deprivation, Mental retardation, Neurological problems (e.g. traumatic brain injury, muscular disease), Facial structural problems, etc.
- **Evaluation** of speech and language delay vary since the causes vary. It includes an Audiologist, Speech Language Pathologist, Paediatrician, developmental paediatrician, neurologist, Ear Nose and Throat specialist, social worker (assess the home environment).
- In the first 5 years of life, the way you engage with your child will determine the path that language development takes. As such, knowing what is "normal" and what is "abnormal" in speech and language development can help you figure out if your child is developing appropriately.

RECOGNIZING SPEECH & LANGUAGE DELAYS

The presentation of speech and language delays can be arranged into three broad categories, which include the following:

Unclear speech (unintelligible)

Speech and language delays or disorders under this category include articulation problems, voice and fluency disorders.

- **Articulation** is the actual mechanical production of speech sounds in sequences to form spoken words. There are 4 types of articulation errors:
  1) **Omission:** The sounds in words and sentences may be completely omitted (e.g. the child may say "I go i bue ca" (I go in blue car).
  2) **Substitutes:** These are characterized by the substitutions of an incorrect sound for a correct one (e.g. the child may say "I saw a wittle wamb", substituting the 'l' sound for the 'w' sound).
  3) **Distortions:** Incorrect and poor sounds result when the child has unsuccessful attempts to produce a proper sound. A distorted sound is not uncommon, since air sometimes escapes from the side of the mouth producing a lateral lisp or distortion. Oral motor errors from the articulators (teeth, tongue, jaw, tongue and lips) compromise sound due to a variety of problems of oral-facial muscles.
  4) **Addition:** These are added vowel or consonant sounds to a single word such as "bananana" for banana, or "pantes" for pants.
- A child with articulation problems will probably omit, substitute, distort or make additions to normal speech sounds at inappropriate ages. For example, it is not unusual for a 3 year old to substitute the "f" sound for the "th" in their speech (e.g. "I am firstly" instead of "I am thirsty"). All sounds are achieved at different ages, and some sound errors may be considered being a developmental delay until the child has reached the expected age for production.

Errors in speech should not occur in a child who is older than 7 years of age; affected children will have some or many inconsistent articulation errors and can progress slowly in speech development, even with speech therapy.

- **Voice disorder** is when an abnormal voice quality, pitch, tone or resonance occurs. This may result from an abnormal larynx (the voice box), which can include vocal chord stress causing scarring or polyps identified by poor vocal quality during phonation at the airway. It can be due to voice misuse or abuse (e.g. habitual screaming or poor vocal hygiene).

With voice disorders, the voice is chronically hoarse, harsh or of poor quality. The pitch in a child with voice disorder may be inappropriate for the child's age and sex. Voice can be characterized with intermittent pitch breaks causing the voice to be hyper nasal with a high strident tone.

- **Fluency disorder** entails problems with the rate and rhythm of speech flow such as stuttering and stammering. With this disorder, signs include sound or word repetitions, sound blocks, sound prolongation disturbing the natural rhythm of speech.

SPEECH DELAYS & CONTENT OF SPEECH

This category includes speech delay or disorder.
- **Speech** is the actual sound of spoken language and is divided into articulation and phonology, voice and fluency.
- **Phonology** is the sound system of language and the rules of sound sequence that make up words. A **phonological disorder** is failing to grow out of patterns such as babbling or developing inappropriate sound patterns.
- **Speech delays** may be noticed when your child does not seem to talk as much as most other children of the same age. Your child's speech skills are developing, but at a much slower rate than normal. Language skills may be age appropriate, but may be seemingly delayed due to the interference of speech errors. For example, the child who experiences speech delays has "his own sounding" vocabulary that is unintelligible to others and suffers with others trying to comprehend the linguistic complexities. The words or message used are accurate but is nonsensical due to being unintelligible. The child may end up speaking in single words, 2-word phrases, and/or incomplete sentences that can be thought of as a language disorder. Some children will choose to use shorter simple phrases if it will be understood easier by the person being spoken to. Having to repeat one self numerous times to be understood can be very tiresome.
- A speech delay can range from being mild, moderate and severe
- A **speech disorder** is manifested when a child's speech skills develop abnormally. When delays persist and affect communicative functions, they become classified as disorders.

    The presentation of a speech disorder may include the following signs:
    - ✓ Deficits in the development of speech skills and voice quality
    - ✓ Problems with the production of speech sounds
    - ✓ Disruptions in the flow or rhythm of speech
    - ✓ Problems with voice, pitch, volume or quality
    - ✓ Poor intelligibility
    - ✓ Phonological disorder

Language Delays

Speech and language delays under this category include children who have difficulty-understanding language (receptive) and/or children who experience difficulty-using language (expressive).

Language delays result when language is developing at a slowing rate, but in the correct sequence.

- Language consists of several parts that develop at the same time and are divided into content, form and use.
    - ✓ **Content** indicates the meaning of a message (i.e. semantic).
    - ✓ **Form** includes syntax and grammar, referring to the rules that define the structure and organization of words into sentences.
    - ✓ **Use** refers to the use of language, both verbal and non-verbal.
- A **receptive language disorder** indicates that a child experiences difficulties understanding the content, form or use of language whereas an **expressive language disorder** poses difficulties for the child to convey a message using content, form or use.
- **Symptoms** of language delays may include:
    - ✓ Fails to meet developmental milestones for language
    - ✓ Language develops falls 1 year behind other child of the same age
    - ✓ Unable to follow directions
    - ✓ Difficulty expressing ideas
    - ✓ Syntax difficulties (i.e. placing words in the correct order to form a sentence)
    - ✓ Misuse of meanings and words
    - ✓ Immature grammatical patterns
    - ✓ Limited vocabulary and comprehension
    - ✓ Punctuated speech with short and non-descriptive sentences
    - ✓ Major gap between non-verbal and verbal abilities
    - ✓ Poor social/emotional pragmatic performance skills
    - ✓ Hearing impairments
- **Pragmatic (i.e. social language) disorder** includes difficulties with conversational skills (e.g. starting, ending and maintaining topics), understanding or using non-verbal forms of communication (e.g. eye contact, body posture, gestures), making or keeping friends and using socially appropriate behaviours.

TIP: Speech & Language Problems – How They Differ
Although problems in speech and language differ, they frequently overlap. For example: 1) A child with a language problem may be able to pronounce words well, but may be unable to put more than 2 words together. 2) Conversely, another child's speech may be difficult to understand, but he may use words and phrases to express ideas. 3) Another child may speak well, but may experience difficulty following directions.

WHAT TO EXPECT: DEVELOPMENTAL MILESTONES FOR SPEECH AND LANGUAGE BY AGE

The following table outlines the typical developmental milestones for speech and language by age, beginning with the newborn up to six years of age. It can help you and your child's health professional decide if your child requires speech and language testing.

	Receptive Skills	Expressive Skills
Birth – 2 Months	<ul><li>Turns to the source of the sound</li><li>Recognizes/prefers familiar voices</li><li>Shows interest in the faces of others</li></ul>	<ul><li>Undifferentiated cry</li></ul>
2 – 4 Months	<ul><li>Turns to you when you speak</li><li>Smiles upon hearing your voice</li><li>Jumps upon hearing loud voices</li><li>Stops activities and attends closely to unfamiliar sounds</li><li>Turns to where a sound is coming from</li></ul>	<ul><li>Coos when content</li><li>Takes turns cooing in response to others cooing</li><li>Randomly babbles</li><li>Smiles at you when you come into view/in response to you</li><li>Uses different cries for different needs (e.g. hunger, pain, etc)</li></ul>
4 – 6 Months	<ul><li>Responds to own name</li><li>Watches your face when you talk</li><li>Fascinated by toys that make sounds</li><li>Enjoys nursery rhymes</li></ul>	<ul><li>Babbles rhythmically</li><li>Makes noises or gestures to get attention</li><li>Makes return sounds when you talk</li><li>Smiles at you and other family members</li></ul>
6 – 12 Months	<ul><li>Understands verbal routines</li><li>Listens when spoken to</li><li>Turns and looks at your face when called by name</li><li>Recognizes the names of familiar objects</li><li>Begins to respond to requests</li></ul>	<ul><li>Points</li><li>Babbles in imitation of real speech with expression</li><li>Babbling sounds change</li></ul>

At **1-2 years of age**, the child learns that smiling and making sounds can affect the behaviour of others. As muscle control is better achieved, the child's communication skills typically progress from vocalization (e.g. grunting, cooing, playing with sounds) and pointing to speaking single/simple words to the conversationalist. At this age, some of the concepts your child should be demonstrating include (a) looking attentively; (b) following simple directions; (c) imitating speech; and (d) asking for simple needs (e.g. drinks, food).

	Receptive Skills	Expressive Skills
12 – 15 Months	<ul><li>Follows verbal commands</li><li>Understands simple instructions</li><li>Recognizes name</li></ul>	<ul><li>Uses jargon (seems like he is talking in sentences, though not real words)</li><li>Imitates familiar sounds (e.g.</li></ul>

			"mama, dada")
			▪ Laughs and tries to make the same sounds you make
			▪ States 1-2 words (need not be clear)
15 – 18 Months	▪ Understands words ▪ Points to body parts by name		▪ Learns words slowly ▪ Makes gestures or asks for more ▪ Asks for repeat (saying "again")
18 – 24 Months	▪ Understands simple sentences, questions and commands ▪ Likes to listen to simple stories and enjoys when you sign a song or say rhymes (by 2 years of age)		▪ Uses 5-20 words including own name ▪ Vocabulary is growing ▪ Learns words quickly ▪ Uses 2-word sentences (e.g. "where ball?" "what that", etc); by 2 years of age

Vocabulary is the ability to produce or understand words. Children typically experience **vocabulary spurts** at 16-24 months of age, ranging from 5-10 words to more than 50 words. During the spurt, your child should acquire 1-2 words per day. When communicating, the child begins with simple words first and then eventually combines these simple words to make sentences.

The language skills of a **2 year old** grow rapidly. However, adults may need to explain many words due to the immature and poor pronunciation skills of a young child. Children at this age understand many simple directions, but cannot yet initiate conversation. Between 2-3 years of age, pronunciation improves considerably, but some sounds are still difficult to master.

	Receptive Skills	**Expressive Skills**
2 – 3 Years	▪ Understands language better ▪ Can answer simple questions (e.g. "what is your name?" "where is the ball", etc) ▪ Understands simple directions and follows 2-step commands (e.g. "put the ball in the box") ▪ Notices the sounds of bells and ringing telephones ▪ Identifies body parts	▪ Builds 2-3 word sentences (e.g. "me do it") ▪ Uses "s" at the end of words when there is more than 1 ▪ Sentences are 50% intelligible ▪ Asks "what" and "why" questions ▪ Engages in short conversations with self and dolls ▪ Articulating consonants more clearly ▪ Combines verbs and nouns ▪ Forms some plurals

From the age of **3 years**, the number of words a child understands is larger than those actually used. There are major improvements in pronunciation and grammar use. At this point, 3-year-old children are able to imitate, initiate and listen in on conversations; however, they are unable to wait for their turn to speak in a group conversation. Children in this age group enjoy sharing personal stories and interests and are generally better in understanding stories and conversations.

	Receptive Skills	Expressive Skills
3 – 4 Years	<ul><li>Understands much of what is said (e.g. understands pictures, shapes, slow/fast, questions, attributes, colours, names)</li><li>Can hear when you call his name from another room</li><li>Listens to stories and answers simple questions</li><li>Has a favourite television program and/or favourite book</li></ul>	<ul><li>Asks "what" and "why" questions</li><li>Speaks clearly so other people can understand what he is saying most of the time</li><li>Uses "I, me, you, she" properly</li><li>Sentences are 75% intelligible</li><li>Masters the early acquired speech sounds (m, b, y, n, w, d, t, p, h) and vowel sounds "a, e, i, o, u"</li><li>Knows nursery rhymes and can tell a song or sing a song</li></ul>

Between **3-4 years of age**, many children experience a period in which the fluency of their output is poor. Some children develop developmental dysfluency or stuttering. **Developmental dysfluency** is characterized by the repetition of whole words and syllables, rather than individual sounds (typically resolved by 4 years of age). **Stuttering** is a long-term speech problem, which consists of the repetition of parts of words, prolongation of sounds and complete blocks. There can be tension and/or a struggle in the attempt to form words.

At **4-5 years of age**, children's language skills are rapidly developing with the increased ability to form complex sentences and few pronunciations errors. Children in this age group can understand given explanations and multi-step directions. A child in this age group, specifically in sharing personal experiences or telling stories, frequently initiates conversations.

	Receptive Skills	Expressive Skills
4 – 5 Years	<ul><li>Understands more of what is said</li><li>Identifies colors and shapes</li><li>Follows 3-step directions (e.g. "stand up and get the ball; give it to me")</li><li>Able to explain the function of objects with better reasoning</li><li>Understands questions and senses (e.g. "what do you do with your eye?")</li></ul>	<ul><li>Creates well-formed sentences</li><li>Tells stories with long and complex sentences (with a clear beginning, middle and end)</li><li>Asks many questions</li><li>Sentence length is 4-5 words (by 5 years of age)</li><li>100% intelligible in speaking clearly and fluently</li><li>Some lisp and difficulties with sounds 'l, r, s, k, th, ch, sh" but this can come later</li><li>Able to communicate easily with familiar adults and with other children</li></ul>
5 – 6 Years	<ul><li>Understands much of what is said</li><li>Identifies coins and understands similar/different</li><li>Understands the meaning of familiar words</li><li>Follows directions (e.g. "give me your pen")</li><li>Knows own address</li><li>Understands spatial relations</li><li>Counts ten items</li></ul>	<ul><li>5-6 word sentences (almost sounding like adults)</li><li>Able to correctly pronounce most speech sounds</li><li>May have difficulty with "sh, th, s, z, l, r" and so forth</li></ul>

LEARNING DISABILITY

Introduction

- **Learning disabilities** refers to a variety of disorders that affect academic and functional skills. About 5-10% of children between the ages of 6-17 years are affected.

- The definition of a **general learning problem** applies to a child with low overall levels of intellectual functioning to acquire school learning skills. A **specific learning disability** is selective learning weakness in a child with average or above average intelligence.
- Children and adults with learning disabilities experience difficulty organizing information. It is manifested by limited school performance (typically after being in school for 2 years), in reading, writing, spelling and mathematics.
- Learning disabilities can affect a wide range of academic and social skills in one or more areas and range from mild to severe. **Problems include the following**:

- ✓ Language (difficulties speaking, listening and writing thoughts or organizing ideas)
- ✓ Reading (poor reading, grammar problems, letter confusion, number reversal, difficulties decoding words)
- ✓ Difficulties with arithmetic and basic number concepts or understanding problems with sequencing and solving problems
- ✓ Difficulties remembering facts & instructions just stated
- ✓ May experience stress due to increased effort
- ✓ Trouble managing time or carrying out a plan / schedule as well as own belongings
- ✓ Difficulties with social adjustment, tolerating frustration and making/keeping friends
- ✓ Problems running and jumping or manipulating small objects
- ✓ High activity level of body and/or hands
- ✓ Problems with knowing, using and monitoring the use of thinking and learning strategies
- ✓ Poor comprehension, slow to acquire skills and experiences visual spatial confusion (e.g. left hand/right hand, under/over)
- ✓ Difficulty differentiating sound

- **Causes** and **risk factors** for underachievement/failures include:
  - ✓ General or specific learning disability
  - ✓ Mental retardation and impaired intellectual ability
  - ✓ ADHD-Attention Deficit Hyperactivity Disorder
  - ✓ Sensory impairment (hearing/vision)
  - ✓ Chronic or emotional illness
  - ✓ Temperament and family dysfunction
  - ✓ Social/cultural and environmental disadvantages
  - ✓ Neurologic dysfunction (infection, injury, disease)

- Learning disability is a lifelong condition; however, with the right support and intervention services, a child with a learning disability can succeed in academics and go on to successful and often, distinguished careers in life.
- The sooner a learning disability is detected and intervention begins, the better the chances are of avoiding school failures, improving future success and production in life, relationships, self-esteem and avoiding frustration, stress and hardships.
- Additionally, parents can help the child achieve success by encouraging his strengths, knowing his weaknesses, understanding the educational system, working with professionals as a team and learning about strategies for dealing with specific difficulties and situations.

PRESENTATION OF LEARNING DISABILITIES

- Children with learning disabilities exhibit a **wide range of symptoms**. No one will have nor requires having all the symptoms for a diagnosis of a learning disability and the number of symptoms might not give an indication as to whether the disability is mild or severe.
- Some symptoms are more common than others among children with learning disabilities. To be considered a warning sign, the child should exhibit the behaviour over time (i.e. chronic) and appear in clusters. This is because every child may occasionally exhibit 1-2 of the symptoms/behaviours.

- A learning disability may first appear as a developmental delay. Yet, many children with developmental delays may catch up with early intervention in special programs and will not present a learning disability.
- At times, a child may experience significant trouble with numbers, letters and speech. While children learn at different rates and with different styles, sometimes the signs are already pronounced at this age. However, in the school years, difficulties with school work and underachievement may signal a more serious learning problem.
- A child with a learning disability may understand a story perfectly well when it is read to him, but will struggle to answer any questions about the story afterwards. Another child may easily recite the alphabet from A-Z, but may be unable to name individual letters when they are pointed out. Yet, still another child may have a hard time putting together puzzles, tying a shoe or buttoning a shirt. Finally, your child may know what he wants to say or write down, but doing so is the actual problem.
- Since it is difficult for children with a learning disability to master certain tasks, they often express frustration, anger, low self-esteem, and sometimes, even depression.
- **Further suspicious signs of a learning disability include:**
  - No unexpected reactions of the child to the learning material (e.g. he may say he never has homework, not prepared to go to school or may spend a lot of time on homework)
  - Complains of pains and vomiting during school days (sign of learning difficulty)
  - Refusal to go to school
  - Extreme behavioural changes in adolescence (e.g. anxiety, tics, anger, mood swings)
  - Motor problems (1/3 of children with learning disabilities have motor problems that are characterized by clumsiness, left/right confusion, eye/hand coordination difficulties, delayed motor skills, etc)
  - Underachievement
  - Educators regularly express concerns about your child's performance and behaviour
  - Certain subject areas are repeatedly below grade level performance
  - Excess hours spend on homework for "just passing" (an unusually high level of effort)
  - Requires constant guidance for tasks or does not understand tasks
  - Easily frustrated with school work
  - Bored, careless and seems withdrawn in class
  - Disorganized, inattentive and sloppy
  - Slow to respond to questions or instructions
  - Physical symptoms of stress (e.g. headache, abdominal pain)
  - Breaks school rules or is loud and disruptive
  - Inappropriately jokes and "clowning"
  - Aggressive towards peers and adult

WARNING SIGNS & SYMPTOMS BY AGE

The following list includes warning signs of a learning disability and symptoms in a child who is suspected and/or diagnosed with a learning disability. You can mark the ones that apply to your child and discuss with your doctor.

The Preschool Child	Language	<ul><li>Difficulties **expressing** himself</li><li>Difficulty learning **new words**</li><li>Problems with **pronunciation** (e.g. cannot sound out letters or remember which letter stands for which sound)</li><li>Poor ability to **follow directions** or routines</li><li>Delay/difficulty **understanding & answering** questions</li><li>**Limited** vocabulary (searching for words)</li><li>**Late talking** compared to other children</li></ul>
	Cognition	<ul><li>Has difficulty **counting, learning** colors, shapes or other concepts</li><li>**Memorizing/learning difficulties** (e.g. of the alphabet, days of the week or numbers).</li></ul>
	Social Behaviour	<ul><li>Difficulties **interacting** with peers or making friends</li><li>May experience sudden **mood changes** in the company of peers</li><li>Easily frustrated</li><li>Temper tantrums</li></ul>
	Attention	<ul><li>Extremely restless (hyperactive)</li><li>Easily distracted</li><li>Short attention span</li></ul>
	Motor skills	<ul><li>Slow to develop fine motor skills</li><li>Difficulties coloring or drawing</li><li>Difficult to grasp or manipulate objects, use scissors, color or paint</li></ul>
The Elementary School Years (learning problems frequently become apparent at this age since there are increasing demands & complex learning tasks)	Language	<ul><li>**Slow learning** (e.g. how letters sound and correspond with one another)</li><li>**Reading and/or spelling** difficulties with errors (e.g. letter reversal – "b/d"; inversion – "m/w"; transpositions – "felt/left"; and substitution – "house/home")</li><li>Problems with **vocabulary** or comprehension (e.g. confusing basic words or using the same word for many things)</li><li>Difficulties **communicating** with others</li></ul>
	Math	<ul><li>Has trouble memorizing math facts or steps of math operations (e.g. memorization table)</li><li>**Confusing math** symbols (e.g. +, -, x)</li><li>Difficulties counting money</li><li>**Reverses** number sequences (e.g. 18/81)</li></ul>

	Cognition	<ul><li>**Slow to learn** new skills</li><li>Unable to follow multiple directions</li><li>Relies heavily on **memorizing** (only wanting to learn one way to solve a problem)</li><li>**Poor recall** of facts (has trouble remembering what someone just said)</li><li>Difficulty with temporal (time) concepts</li></ul>
	Motor Skills	<ul><li>Poor handwriting</li><li>Difficulties aligning columns</li><li>Awkward, poor coordination</li><li>Prone to accidents</li></ul>
	Attention	<ul><li>Impulsive and lack of planning</li><li>Difficulties concentrating or completing work on time</li></ul>
	Social behaviour	<ul><li>Difficulties making friends</li><li>Struggles with organization and self-esteem</li></ul>
The High School Student/Adult		<ul><li>**Avoids** reading and writing tasks</li><li>**Misreads** information</li><li>Difficulties summarizing information</li><li>Continues having **trouble** with spelling, which is often incorrect</li><li>**Poor grasp** of abstract concepts</li><li>Has trouble with **open-ended questions** on tests</li><li>Weak memory skills (poor short-term or long-term memory)</li><li>Either pays **too little attention** to details or focuses on some too much</li><li>Difficulties with **abstract reasoning** and/or problem solving</li><li>**Impulsive** behaviour and **low tolerance** for frustration</li><li>Difficulties with tasks requiring sequencing</li><li>**Easily confused** by instructions</li><li>Behaviour is often **inappropriate** for a situation, often being excessive displays of affection or failure to understand the consequences of an action</li><li>**Frequent changes in mood and social responses**</li><li>Difficulties **adjusting** to new situations</li></ul>

CPSIA information can be obtained at www.ICGtesting.com
Printed in the USA
LVOW070855180612

286509LV00003B/7/P